# Three Neo-Noir Thriller Stage Plays

(based on the screenplays)

by

Karl J. Niemiec

Noir Pictures
NoirPic55@gmail.com

# Three Neo-Noir Thriller Stage Plays



ISBN 978-0983366393

Published by LapTop Publishing - Karl J. Niemiec

Printed and bound in the United States of America.

For production rights to any of these three plays, please contact Karl J. Niemiec at: NoirPic55@gmail.com

For more books, games, plays and screenplays by Karl J. Niemiec, please visit: LapTop Publishing @ http://amzn.to/karlniemiec

# Table of Contents

## Going Bad 4

**A Detroit Neo-Noir Mob Thriller**

Five thieves weave a deviantly twisted love-torn plot, to rob a depraved, old-school killer, leaving a handsome med student's life in ruins, waiting for the evil he knows will someday seek what they stole.

## When The Right Man Finds You 83

**A Tragic Romantic Thriller**

A gifted couple with shadowy pasts fall passionately in love while restoring a turn-of- the-century-old mansion—only to discover that some secrets won't stay buried, and their dream home may become their grave.

## *Bonjour, America* 161

**A Neo-Noir Sensory-Immersive Thriller**

Small town, big crime, 1960 - French suit Salesman, Vincent Boyer holds the money a bad cop killed for, when all he wants is to get home in time to save his American family, but must first overcome his greatest fears to stay alive.

**Note from the Author: as written these stories are vivid with sex, action, and violence, but they can be directed, toned, and staged in anyway that fits your venue to tell these stories full heartedly, including with minimal sets, lighting, and yes... with or without an old dog.**

## What is a Neo-Noir story?

Neo-noir (English: New-black; from the Greek neo, new; and the French noir, black) is a style often seen in modern motion pictures and other forms that prominently utilize elements of film noir, but with updated themes, content, style, visual elements, or media that were absent in films noir of the 1940s and 1950s.

## About the Author:

I write love stories in multiple genres and live with my family of six in Carmel, Indiana.

After moving from Los Angeles in 2006, I became an Adjunct Professor at IUPUI. I taught from my popular course books, Write to be Published and The Inside Pitch recommended How to be a Prolific Screenwriter developed at UCLA Extension.

I was then hired to direct 9 wildly parent acclaimed children's summer musicals, which led to teaching children, teens, and adults at KjN Studio, an on-camera technique inspired from private training inside ABC's Film Library, before casting me out of the mailroom and offering me a role on General Hospital and Welcome Back Kotter. I had the run of ABC by the head of Prospect Lot and given permission to sit in any job and learn what they were doing. And I did. I even got kicked out an editing session by Alivia Newton John because she didn't know I was invited and felt uncomfortable since she hadn't seen the footage yet.

Five of these scenes from my published book, Audition Monologues that Work, were accepted as IMBd credits and two were selected into Film Festivals. Three of which, premiered right here in Indy at The Box Film Studio, where Indiana Film Network holds its monthly meetings.

This led to a National Manager/Agent Audition Showcase flying me to LA twice a year to direct actor reels and shoot the entire events.

These adventures inspired me to reformat screenplays into stage plays, novels, and audiobooks, using the same reformatting technique in How to be a Prolific Screenwriter, resulting in these ***Three Neo-Noir Thriller Stage Plays.***

*Karl J. Niemiec*

# GOING BAD

**A Neo-Noir Thriller Stage Play**

**(based on the screenplay)**

**by**

Karl J. Niemiec

# CHARACTERS

**DOC MITCHELL:** Black, thirties, almost finished his residency before getting shot up bad and left a cripple during a heist. Plays both a the crippled and healthy character.

**JIM STOCK:** Thirties, white trash flunky thief and a sucker. Works with Jules. (Note: Would work well to cast twins because of makeup and staging. Or two look alike actors.

**LEON POE:** Forties. East Coast Gangster. Looking for what he believes to be half his.

**CHAZZ COLSON:** Forties, Evil East Coast Gangster. Driver for the Old Man, who is looking for what he believes to be half his after being shot in the chest during the heist.

**CORRINE:** Asian, early twenties. Has the body men pay good money to watch and kill to own, with a face and mouth that knows it. Using Jules more than he's using her.

**DONNA CONNOLLY:** Black, early thirties, seen enough. Apartment manager, tall, slender, tries to look good, but is an unsatisfied bitter bitch over getting jolted by Doc after the heist went bad, and left with his school debt and a truck driver roommate.

**JULES STIMEN:** Later forties, and still a small time New York born fence ,now hiding in Detroit, and doing his best to hang onto and use Corrine for something big. Lives part time on someone else's boat in a harbor on the Detroit River.

**OLD MAN:** An old-school killer, but depraved, and now delusional, racked with guilt, claiming he killed Kennedy and cleaned up the murder of Hoffa and many others. In a fit of a mushroom hallucination, he asks Doc to take what he made from his sins to his mother's church and donate it in her maiden for having a child like him.

**EDDIE SÁNCHEZ:** Thirties. Doing okay, a hanger-on, selling stuff to Jules. Patch over an eye. Airport baggage handler by day, petty thief by trade.

**BULLHEAD LENNY BULCOWKI:** Black, sixties, drunk, ex-hospital custodian where Doc last worked.

**BARTENDER:** Black. Sixties. Just this side of a drunk himself. Played by same actor that plays Bullhead.

**MARGE NELSON:** Any race. Fifties. Nurse at hospital where Doc worked.

**SETTINGS:**

A Neo-Noir with minimal stagging, set in Detroit with a harbor, lake or bay, Henry Ford Hospital, and old Mansion. The feel is dangerous, hot, and gritty. A dark and sexually twisted existence of what bad money does to weak and desperate people.

Two complete dramas unfold on stage in Multiple Flashbacks of Five Years Ago and Present Day scenes. Both then-and-now scenes take place on stage simultaneously and are shown with simple lights up and to black, or can be done pre-recorded V.O., for fluent stagging.

This is done as segues between scene and simple act changes to allow actors to go from one location to the next and back as both Flashback and Present Day Stories continue to unfold at multiple locations within scenes.

**TIME:**

In the heat of the Summer five years into the past and a cool rainy present Fall night. Done in multiple flashbacks, told to stay alive, about what happened from each character's point of view, whether telling the truth or not. Sets can be stark, using lights to separate multiple settings. The desperation, sex ,and violence between the characters are the thing.

**ACTS - SCENES:**

**ACT I - Scene One -** Warehouse District Deadbeat Bar - Night
**ACT I - Scene Two -** Ext. Detroit Apartments - Night
**ACT I - Scene Three -** The Coffee Can - Present Day - Night
**ACT I - Scene Four -** Int. Henry Ford Hospital - Night
**ACT I - Scene Five -** Jules' boat - Night

**ACT II - Scene One -** Ext. Grounds - Old Man's house - Night
**ACT II - Scene Two -** Int. The Coffee Can - Night
**ACT II - Scene Three -** Int. The Coffee Can - Night
**ACT II - Scene Four -** Int. Corrine's Home - Bedroom - Night
**ACT II - Scene Five -** Darkened Marina Parking Lot - Night

**At Rise**

**ACT I**
**Scene One**

**Lights up. Int. Warehouse District Deadbeat Bar - 11 p.m.**

CHAZZ COLSON, 40's in a hat and overcoat enters the local deadbeat bar.

The grizzled BARTENDER, 60s just this side of a drunk himself, is closing down for the night. His eyes asking nothing.

Chazz moves to the bar.

CHAZZ
Two shots. That bottle.

BARTENDER
(back to him, cleaning)
Sorry, pal wrong place. Just about to lock....
(sees Chazz's reflection in the mirror...)

Chazz opens his coat, showing the Bartender what he's got.

Fearful, the Bartender grabs and turns, not meeting eyes, to pour the two shots. He goes to put the bottle back....

...when LEON POE, 40s, hat and overcoat, steps up behind him and takes his wrist and makes him leave the bottle on the bar.

LEON
We're looking for a man used to go by Doc Mitchell. Works here.

BARTENDER
I don't....

Leon applies pressure to the Bartender's arm.

CHAZZ
One body-two bodies... it don't make no difference.

BARTENDER
Woman who owns this joint... hires a gimpy guy to --

CHAZZ
-- That's him.

BARTENDER
I don't know him by that name, but he's either in a heap out back, or in the can.

Leon motions for the Bartender to pour them both another round. They down it.

LEON
Anyone else work here?

BARTENDER
Not tonight.

Leon and Chazz head for the can at the back of the bar. Chazz motions for the men's room door. Chazz reveals a sawed-off twelve gage pump as they go in.

**Lights to Black**

**Lights Up in single stall Men's Room**

As Leon and Chazz enter and stand in front of the stall with two beat up, but nice shoes under the door.

CHAZZ
We got a question for you?

BULLHEAD (O.S.)
Get out, I'm takin' a dump, here.

LEON
Where's the old man's five mil?

BULLHEAD (O.S.)
Yeah right, piss off?

LEON
You remember who we are?

BULLHEAD (O.S.)
Yeah, a couple of inconsiderate assholes. Now give a man his moment.

Bullhead kicks the stall door startling Chazz as it swings open and Chazz's shotgun goes off, splattering yuck back on them.

CHAZZ
You've had it, Doc.

LEON
Ah shit, Chazz.

The two men put away their guns.

LEON
Some fun in the sun.

CHAZZ
And we still got two whole days.

Leon spits. He looks around for a mirror.

CHAZZ
There ain't one.

LEON
I got anything in my teeth?

CHAZZ
Just a little.

LEON
Doc had a point, you know. Maybe we should'a asked him a few Q's before we blew his head off.

CHAZZ
I got five years of kissing boss-ass and a slug in the chest from one of those pricks. I don't need to take Q's from any of them. We search Doc's shit, we'll find the others. And what's left of our money.

LEON
(continues cleaning. his teeth and suit)
As long as you're paying the dry cleaning. Here, I got this out of the heap out back.
(takes out a letter, holds it up for Chazz)

Chazz takes it and pulls out a photo of a woman.

CHAZZ
From a girlfriend. Donna. Not the one he had with him that night. Posted four years ago. This address is probably where Doc grew up.
(hands letter back to Leon)
To his mother. She needed money. Cross town address. No phone.

LEON
Yeah, and from the looks of his heap she didn't get any.

CHAZZ
Maybe the other ones. Let's ask.

Chazz and Leon exit the men's room.

**Lights to Black**

**End of ACT I**
**Scene One**

**ACT I**
**Scene Two**

**Lights Up on Ext. Old Detroit Apartments/Veranda**

Cold and gloomy - Night. The brick apartments have a front veranda with a table and chairs beside the front door.

Leon and Chazz look up the name on the call box. They find who they're looking for and BUZZ. They still wear their overcoats.

DONNA (V.O.
Do you know what time it is?

CHAZZ
We're friends of Doc Mitchell.

DONNA (V.O.)
Who?

CHAZZ
Doc Mitchell. We'd like to speak to you about him.

DONNA (V.O.)
I haven't seen or heard from the bastard in five years.

CHAZZ
He worked downtown picking up drunks... takin' them home.

DONNA (V.O.)
So what?

CHAZZ
He's dead.

DONNA (V.O.)
I'll be right out.

DONNA CONNOLLY, 30's, opens the front door. Tall, slender, fairly good looking... unsatisfied. A bitch.

DONNA
My friend works nights. Why don't we talk out here?
(Donna walks onto the apartment veranda)
You guys from county?

LEON
Sometimes.

DONNA
He leave a will?

CHAZZ
We're looking into it.

Chazz pulls a chair for Donna to sit. Leon lights her cigarette as he and Chazz pull chairs and get comfy.

CHAZZ
Nice place.

LEON
You own it?

DONNA
No. How'd you find him?

CHAZZ
Drunk named Bullhead.

Donna offers a cigarette. They decline.

DONNA
Lenny Bulcowski... custodian where Doc worked.

CHAZZ
That's him. When was the last time you heard from Doc?

DONNA
Like I said, five years ago.

Chazz takes out the letter. She looks at it, reaching... opens it... looks at the photo.

DONNA
I needed money for his school bills. His mother claimed she didn't know where he was.

LEON
Guess she was lying.

DONNA
Screw her, she's dead.

CHAZZ
Glad to see you're not bitter.

DONNA
Who are you guys?

CHAZZ
Do you recall any of his friends? Someone he might have met just before --

DONNA
-- I want to know who you guys are.

LEON
We want to know what Doc did with all the money.

DONNA
Money? What money? I put his ass through med school while he babysat his momma. Was there money?

CHAZZ
That's what we want to know.

DONNA
What makes it any business of yours?

LEON
We're making it.

DONNA
I don't have a clue to what you guys are talking about. So please, don't waste my time with bullshit.
(stands, stub cig, to leave))
Doc never had money, believe me. And the little he had went to his momma. All the expense and pain she had... should've just put her crabby ass to sleep.

CHAZZ
(gets up like he's about to leave)
Then I guess if we find it... you won't be interested.

Leon gets up, checking the neighborhood.

DONNA
Wait a minute... if there is --

Chazz suddenly grabs her by the throat.

CHAZZ
-- It's ours!

Chazz squeezes, cutting off all her air. Every time she grabs for his hands, he squeezes harder. Chazz and Leon look at each other as they wait. Leon checks his watch. He doesn't want to kill this one.

LEON
She's close.

CHAZZ
Couple more.

They wait. Chazz let's up. She gasps for air as she gets put into the chair.

CHAZZ
Next time I snap it.

She sits gasping, pissed, but even more scared. Leon and Chazz sit back down.

LEON
Secluded, this part of the block. Quiet.

DONNA
You killed him, didn't you?

CHAZZ
What happened to Doc and you?

Donna eyes her cigarettes. Leon takes one and lights it, puts it into her mouth. She inhales. Leon and Chazz wait. She exhales... and it pours out... fighting not to cry... all this time, needing to tell it to someone.

DONNA
Doc almost finished his residency. He hadn't asked me to marry him. I understood he was waiting... for his mother to pass on. We didn't.... The last time I saw him he came home bleeding badly from the side. And he couldn't move his left arm. Blood dripping from his fingers. He packed a few things, clothes, and took off. He quit everything... me, his mother. Just dropped out of our lives. His mother got by somehow... maybe he helped, I don't know. The dirty rotten... shit, he loved her, do anything... but I loved him, you know.

CHAZZ
And you just let him go like that?

DONNA
He wouldn't let me help him.

CHAZZ
So maybe he found help somewhere else?

DONNA
There was another woman. Corrine... I can't remember the little tramp's last name. But she was no nurse's aide, or candy striper, or whatever she was pretending to be. The bitch. Young, beautiful, a friend of hers had money. Lived on a boat... Jules. I met Doc there once for drinks after he'd gotten off work. Doc had a lot of energy... but not money... just dreams. She played him for a sucker. Probably right from the start.

CHAZZ
How so?

DONNA
She had tits... all right? And knew the value of them. Those others, there was something about those crumbs. They weren't like Doc. I didn't trust any of them.

LEON
Why?

DONNA
Because I didn't like them. Because I thought they were thieves. So I had Doc stay away from them. He did too, for awhile. Then he started coming home late again, and we'd fight. He may have screwed the little.... She went both ways... that I do know.

CHAZZ
Uh-huh....

**Black on Present Day**

**Lights Up on Donna's Flashback**

Detroit - Harbortown Marina. Five years ago - Night. Secluded boat dock, MUSIC drifts up from the deck of a twenty-four foot cabin cruiser. It's nice, but far from new.

CORRINE, mid-20s, shoes off, the kind of body men pay good money to watch, and kill to own.

She dances slowly to the soft MUSIC in white stockings on the deck of the cruiser. She still has her hospital work clothes on... provocatively unbuttoned.

JULES STIMEN, 50's, New York Thief, pours drinks.

DOC MITCHELL, 29, strapping young med student, and Donna sit together at a table at the stern of the boat. Donna has a drink. Five years younger, not as hard. Doc has bottled water... watching Corrine.

JIM STOCK 30's, white trash flunky and petty thief, climbs out of the cabin, snotting his nose from blow.

JULES

Jim, grab a bottle of tonic around the corner. Sure you don't want another one, Doc?

Jim reaches for the tonic. Hands it to Jules, as he dances over to sit next to Donna. Jim smiles at her. Coke crumbs on his nose.

DOC

I'll end it with this.

JIM

You want to dance?

DONNA

(sees the coke crumbs)

Thanks, no.

JIM

How about you, Doc?

Jules moves over and hands Corrine a drink. She kisses him. He sits at the table.

JULES

Shut up, Jim. You must see some real shit down there at Ford Emergency.

DOC
Very real.

CORRINE
Tell them how they stitched the wrong hand on the guys wrist.

JULES
That must've cost a bundle.

DOC
It was on purpose.

JIM
At least he could still jerk off.

JULES
(sees the coke crumbs)
Dance with Corrine.

Jim gets up and dances over to Corrine. She turns her back to the others. And secretly licks the coke crumbs from Jim's nose. Jim just about wets his pants.

JULES
I try to avoid dead people. You know what I mean?

DOC
So do I, Jules.

JULES
Dead or alive, somebody pays the bill. Right?

DOC
It's a good racket.

DONNA
It's not just about the money. I mean, it can't be... just that.

DOC
There's the people.

JULES
So, you into medicine, Donna?
(something catches Jules' attention)

DONNA
Administration... I, ah --

JULES
(gets up)
-- Excuse me.
(goes down below)

EDDIE SÁNCHEZ, 30's, enters. He has a patch over an eye. Dressed in a Detroit Metro Airport baggage handler uniform. He carries an expensive RIFLE CASE and jumps aboard.

EDDIE
Sorry to interrupt.

He dances past Corrine and Jim, following Jules into the cabin. Donna leans close to Doc.

DONNA
Let's go home.

DOC
In a minute.

JIM
(moves back to the table)
Dance with her, Doc.

Corrine motions Doc out to her. Doc looks at Donna then gets up to dance. Pulling her up with him. They move over to dance with Corrine.

Donna is slow to get into it. Gradually the three of them blend. Donna not wanting to dig it. But does.

Jules comes out of the cabin followed by Eddie. Eddie is putting money into his pocket. Eddie pinches Corrine as he goes to the bar.

Jules moves over to the table, watching them dance.

JULES
You get tired?

JIM
She told me to sit down.

JULES
Hey, Doc, come here?

Doc dances over to Jules. Leaving Corrine and Donna together for a moment. Donna looks a little uncertain. Corrine takes her hands.

CORRINE

Just this song.

They continue to dance. Donna playing shy.

EDDIE

Yum, do that thing you do, girls.

Doc sits across from Jules. They watch the women dance.

JULES

Medical supplies... interesting business.

DOC

I suppose.

JULES

You must know a lot about that stuff.

DOC

I'm not ripping any off, if that's what you're asking.

JULES

Oh, you mean that. Eddie's dad needed money. Eddie, come here. This is Doc Mitchell. That's his girl, Donna.

EDDIE

Dances nice. I got to get back to work, Jules.

JULES

Tell your dad I said thanks.

EDDIE

Huh, oh, yeah, sure... later gators.

Eddie takes off as the song ends. Donna moves over to get her purse. She's disturbed.

DONNA

We have to go.

DOC

In a minute, honey.

DONNA
I have to work in the morning. And you pick up your mother. Nice meeting you all.

Donna glances at Corrine. Nothing pleasant there. She heads for the docks.

DOC
Well, I guess we're out of here. Nice meeting you, Jules... Jim. Corrine, I'll see you at work.

CORRINE
Bye... she's interesting, Doc.

They exchange looks as Doc goes. Corrine, still dancing, turns to face Jules as Doc goes after Donna.

JULES
What did you say to her?

CORRINE
Just girl talk.

**Black out on Donna' Flashback**

**Lights Up on Present Day - Continuing**

In front of Donna's apartment building. Donna stubs out her cig. Leon and Chazz are all ears.

DONNA
In fact, the one called Jim, owns a coffee shop not far from here. On the boulevard, a couple of months ago, there was an article when his place opened up. The Coffee Can.

CHAZZ
And you went to see him?

DONNA
Yes, of course. He remembered me.

LEON
And?

DONNA
He'd been in prison.

CHAZZ
Where'd he get the money?

DONNA
Why ask me?

LEON
What about the others?

DONNA
After Doc came and went, I drove to where the boat was. Someone set it on fire. The dock master didn't know anyone by the name of Jules. The boat was registered to someone else.

CHAZZ
Who?

DONNA
He wouldn't tell me... I swear... it was a police matter. I was afraid for Doc, so I didn't push. He was never the same after meeting them... especially her... Corrine... they screwed up my life. I'm sleeping with a dumbass truck driver.

CHAZZ
Sounds like it.

LEON
Don't make us come back.

DONNA
Don't worry, I won't.

**End of ACT I**
**Scene Two**

**ACT I**
**Scene Three**

**Lights Up on The Coffee Can - Present - Night.**

Chazz takes a Detroit News from the trash can. He looks around and enters the shop, turning The "open" sign to "closed" as he shuts the door. Chazz crosses from the door. Leon comes in from the back.

Jim Stock is behind the counter GRINDING coffee. He doesn't hear them.

Jim turns to find the two gangsters sitting at each end of his counter. Jim smiles... worried. He shuts off the grinder.

JIM

Am I in a shit load?

CHAZZ

Not yet.

JIM

Give me a minute. My girl has an audition... so I'm fillin' in. You try to run a business... it's showbiz... what can you do? Singers, you know... they gotta do. Besides she's so cute. So I....

Chazz opens the paper, blocking view of Jim from the street, while Leon makes his way around the counter.

Jim makes a move for a bat above the cash register.

But Leon grabs Jim by the back of the head. And forces his face down under the steamer nozzle. Holding it there just above the eye.

JIM

What is this, a shake down? Take whatever you want.

CHAZZ

We just came in to read the paper. Have a cap. Talk about old times.

JIM

We know each other?

CHAZZ

Doc Mitchell. Our mutual friend.

JIM

You're mistaken. I never heard of him.

LEON

(steams Jim's forehead)

That must'a hurt bad.

CHAZZ

I wonder what a machine like that would do to an eye? Heard you had a friend missing an eye. Guy named Eddie... worked out at the airport.

Leon positions Jim's eye under the steamer.

JIM

I swear I don't know anything.

Chazz continues to read his paper. Leon pulls down on the lever. Jim SCREAMS. Leon has his big paw around Jim's throat. Pinning his back to the counter with a knee under his groin. Forcing him under the STEAM. Burning the hell out of Jim's eye. Chazz eventually looks up from his paper.

CHAZZ
Check it.

Leon positions Jim's right eye under the steamer.

CHAZZ
That looks bad. Poached even. You should see a doctor.

LEON
You see any docs lately, Jimbo?

JIM
(eye is boiled shut)
I swear, I ain't seen him in years.

LEON
Too late, he's dead.

JIM
I'm not surprised.

CHAZZ
We heard you, a girl, and two other guys were great party friends of Doc's.

JIM
Who killed him?

CHAZZ
We did.

LEON
And we'll do the same for you, but real slow unless you tell us what you know.

JIM
Okay, okay.

CHAZZ
Get him some ice.

Leon gives ice in a towel to Jim.

CHAZZ
Start talking.

JIM
Shit, I'm blinded in this eye.

LEON
It's better than being dead in both.

CHAZZ
Ask Doc.

JIM
Sure, we met Doc. And his girl.

LEON
That would be Donna.

JIM
Yeah, out on Jules Stimen's boat. A whole stinkin' life ago.

**Black out on Present Day**

**Lights Up on Jim's Flashback**

Ext. Jules' Boat - Five years ago - Jim's story - Night. Just before Doc and Donna arrive for the first time. Jim takes a long hit of coke from a deck table.

JIM
So, what's with this doctor?

JULES
Corrine says he's interesting.

JIM
She doin' him?

JULES
It's business.

JIM
One and the same.

JULES
He's bringing his girl. Keep your trap shut when they get here. Don't want to spook 'em.

JIM
Corrine dumpin' bedpans...? Come on. What's the angle? Drugs?

JULES
Medical supplies.

JIM
You think you can work him?

JULES
If he's workable.

JIM
Big dough.

JULES
I know a guy lookin' for machines. The big stuff. Wants to hit the delivery trucks. He needs someone on the inside above reproach.

JIM
Like a doctor.

JULES
You ain't as thick as you look, Jim.

JIM
Yeah, I dropped some.... Thanks.
(feelings hurt)

**Black on Jim's Flashback**

**Lights Up on Present Day - Continuing**

Inside The Coffee Can - Night.

JIM
Donna only came just that once. She was a bitch anyway.

LEON
Yeah, we met. She had fond memories of you, too.

JIM
Screw her. She came in here... gave me a hard time.

CHAZZ
We don't care.

JIM
Doc didn't come back for awhile... Jules thought we scared him off. But Corrine kept workin' him at the hospital. Man this girl had it. Out to here. Jesus, I miss those days... hate them even more.

LEON
You can fantasize later.

JIM
Sorry... like I said....

**Black on Present Day**

**Lights Up on Jim' Flashback - Continuing**

Ext.Bar - Night. Doc waits at a table. Corrine crosses the street to him. Doc looks a little confused. She's out of uniform.

CORRINE
Hey, Doc, you been avoiding me?

DOC
Of course not. My mother, she's been... well, she's not doing so good. So, I've... how've you been?

CORRINE
So-so. What's new with the girlfriend?

DOC
Working hard... but good. You look rather--

CORRINE
-- exhausted. I know.

DOC
Shouldn't have to work so hard.

CORRINE
And I thought strippin' was shitty work. I count bedpans in my sleep.
(takes a cigarette out)
I know you've got to go. But could we stay for a few?

DOC
What about your shift?

CORRINE
I got someone to cover for me.

DOC
This table okay?

CORRINE
Sure, I just need someone to talk to.
(sits bringing her chair closer)

DOC
I'm a surgeon not a shrink.

CORRINE
You're smart so you'll do.
(takes a sip from Doc's drink)
Sorry, I needed that real bad.

DOC
Don't be, my second. Finish it. What's up?

CORRINE
Jules, that second-rate prick. I'm having troubles dealing with him. Making me work like this, jotting notes about stuff I don't give a crud about.

DOC
So, why don't you just leave him?

CORRINE
He'd never let me go.

DOC
You're a big girl. Just take off.

CORRINE
And go where?

DOC
Anywhere. You'd look good on the back of a milk carton.

CORRINE
I'm not jokin' around, Doc. Come on. That's his Beamer I drive. I live in his condo. I spend his money.

DOC
Take a train or bus.

CORRINE
Alone?

DOC
If you have to.

CORRINE
You don't know Jules.

DOC
I guess I don't.

CORRINE

Help me, Doc. I'm going crazy. You know what a town like Detroit can do to a girl built like me. I was strippin' privately when I was twelve. Jules has video and he's talkin' about postin' them on one of them web pages... you know, the dirty ones... something about passive income.

DOC

What can I do?

Corrine's lips are close to Doc's. Her chest on his arm.

CORRINE

I don't know, something. At least make my life more interesting.

DOC

Interesting?

CORRINE

Jules will never be man enough for me. The way that I see it. I've got all these pent up images in my head. You know?

DOC

I can understand.

CORRINE

Do you?

DOC

But there's Donna. We're --

CORRINE

-- I know. She's got a nice ass.

DOC

So you did hit on her.

CORRINE

Think about it.

DOC

Believe me, I am. I've been with Donna for a long time, though. I couldn't do that to her... and my mom and I, we owe Donna a lot.

CORRINE

Maybe it's time you gave Donna something special. Like me.

**Black on Jim's Flashback**

**End of ACT I**
**Scene Three**

**ACT I**
**Scene Four**

**Lights stay Black**

JIM (V.O.)
I'm just tellin' you what she told us. So, Doc's back around... when about a month or so goes by. Me, Jules, Corrine, and even Eddie was there listin' to him tell it.

DOC (V.O.)
... this limo pulls up outside. And some old man is helped out by his driver. So, we put him on a gurney. The old man's clutching his chest, in awful pain. We all thought classic cardiac. Only the driver starts yelling for us to move faster, get him off the street. I don't know who's more hysterical the driver, the old man, or the nurse the driver threatened.

**Lights Up on Jim's Flashback - Continuing**

Int. Henry Ford Hospital reception area - Doc's Story-Night.

Chazz, then a DRIVER, is at the hospital reception. MARGE NELSON, 50's, a nurse takes his personal information.

Doc exits a room up the hall. Passing by a custodian, LENNY BULCOWKI, "Bullhead", 40's, sweeping floor.

MARGE
I need to know his name. Or I can't admit him.

CHAZZ
That's my name right there. That's our address. That's all you need to know.

MARGE
I'm sorry, sir.

CHAZZ
Yes, you will be, Marge.

Marge picks up the phone. Chazz glances and catches Lenny looking.

MARGE
I'll have none of that. I'll call....

Chazz takes her hand. Places the phone down. Slowly twists her wrist. He opens his coat. Shows her something. Lenny, sees this, turns away, and walks away.

CHAZZ
This is a very delicate matter.

DOC
(walks to the counter)
Excuse me, sir.

CHAZZ
Back off.

DOC
It's about your associate.

CHAZZ
He's dead?

DOC
No. He's fine now. We pumped his stomach. Mushrooms.

CHAZZ
What?

DOC
Fly agaric - a psychoactive mushroom. He was hallucinating.

CHAZZ
He's not dying?

DOC
No. He's fine. But they're also poisonous, with dangerous side effects, so I'd like to keep him here over night. For observation just in case.

CHAZZ
If he's fine, I'll take him home.

DOC
He wants to stay here. With me.

CHAZZ
I don't know about that.

DOC
He's scared... thought he was dying. I'm happy to spend the night. I've reading to do... and I'm off tomorrow.

CHAZZ
I'll need to talk to him.

DOC
Fine. Up there... second door on the left.

Chazz walks O.S. leaving Marge with Doc.

MARGE
He has a gun.

DOC
It's his business.

MARGE
He wouldn't give me the man's name. I'm calling the police.

DOC
Do me a favor, will you, Marge. Put him in a room by himself, for me. He's an interesting old fart. I want to talk to him. And please no police.

**Black on Jim's Flashback - Doc's Story**

**Lights Up on Jim's Flashback - Continuing**

Jules' Boat - Night. Eddie gets up to get a drink.

EDDIE
Wait a minute... anyone else want a drink?

JIM
Me.

EDDIE
So you wanted to stay with this guy? Even though you knew his Mook was packin'?

DOC (V.O.)
I felt for the guy... it might'a just been crap, but earlier...

**Black on Jim's Flashback**

**Lights Up - Hospital - Doc's Story - Continuing**

Doc and the Old Man are left alone. The Old Man is strapped to a bed. He's delirious with fear, guilt, and mushrooms. Doc fills out his chart.

OLD MAN
Come here... please come here.

DOC
You're fine.

OLD MAN
I'm a dead man, Doc. You hear me?

DOC
Not tonight.

OLD MAN
She tried to kill me.

DOC
Who did?

OLD MAN
The one with the big tits.

DOC
She's not here now.

OLD MAN
I was paying her... I couldn't breath, my chest, my heart... promise me --

DOC
-- You're in a hospital. We've pumped your stomach. You'll be fine in the morning.

OLD MAN
You got to promise me something. Promise me you'll go to my home. There's a suitcase. Over five mil. Upstairs under the floor in the master bedroom. I'm not a good man. You should know that. I've sinned all my life and I'm gonna end up in hell for sure. I've sold my soul. Many, many years ago when I was just a dumb kid.

DOC
Okay, let's save this one for our follow up visit.

OLD MAN

You got to fix it for me. You're good, they'll listen to you. Take the money, all of it, to St. Michael's... back home... my driver knows the place. But don't tell why. Go to confession. Father Donovan... he knows what I want. Leave it there. A shrine and a grant in my mother's name. Her maiden name... the name her father gave her. She was ashamed of me. How bad does a boy got to get so his own mother can't stand to see his face? This is the face. You're lookin' at that face. I've changed the world. With these hands. I've killed so many people. Important people. Good people... some not so good. Some deserved it. But I done it for money. Millions. For that money. Take it all. No one knows about it. Take it all. Give it to him. Promise me.

DOC

I promise. If you don't wake up tomorrow... I'll do like you asked. Okay?

OLD MAN

Stay with me. I can't trust nobody. There's no good around me, just evil. Please, I'm dying

DOC

You're fine. At this rate you'll probably out live me. We'll put you in a nice safe --

OLD MAN

You'll stay with me?

DOC

Ah --

OLD MAN

-- Please. I got nobody who cares. No family. No friends... nobody.

DOC

What about your driver?

OLD MAN

Him? He's just like me. Evil. A vulture, waiting for me to go.

DOC

Okay, I'll stay with you.

OLD MAN

Thank you... thank you... go tell him. Tell him I'm staying with you tonight.

**Black on Jim's Flashback - Doc's Story**

**Lights Up on Jim's Flashback - Continuing**

Jules' Boat - Night. Jules is pouring drinks.

CORRINE
Hey, don't forget me.

JULES
I asked.

CORRINE
Well, I didn't hear.

JULES
(makes Corrine a drink)
Christ. Mushrooms, huh? Like 'em.

JIM
So who was this guy?

EDDIE
He said he didn't know. Remember the other guy filled the paperwork.

JIM
It was one of them rhetorical questions, dummy.

EDDIE
Rhetorical this?

JULES
This is gettin' interesting, so shut up, the rest of ya.

**Back on Jim's Flashback**

**Lights Up on Jim's Flashback - Doc's Story Continuing**

Doc is startled awake by the Old Man BABBLING in his sleep.

OLD MAN
... then there was Jerry Steinberg. I was fourteen... no twelve... I shot him in the back, six times. Never saw his eyes... never look them in the eyes they told me... don't feel. I killed a hooker once... no twice... just for kicks. Do' em and kill 'em, I don't know why.

Doc gets up to check the Old Man's pulse and eyes.

OLD MAN

In the war... the big one... I killed hundreds of men, women and children. I dropped bombs. Big ones. I liked it. No eyes. I was a good killer... I'm a pro. Big man... I shot Kennedy. Never met him. Big political job. Pissed the wrong people off. Money people. Not by myself... but I got him. And Hoffa... that dumb son-of-a-bitch... his big mouth... sorry, Father... I cremated him... and his friend. I didn't kill 'em, but I cleaned 'em for... I never liked him anyway... burning... then I killed the others, the one who shot him, young kid, and the others who drove. Truck drivers. You see that movie? Daffy Hollywood. Never knew their names. I had to... nobody could know but me... just me. I got all the money. You can't tell? So I'm telling you, Father. Someone must know, someone must speak for me in the end. So God will understand. Please don't cry. In the end, won't he kill all his children? Isn't one soul as bad as millions? I've made millions, Father... millions. How much will it cost... because of me... to save the mother who had me? A boy like me? I made millions... millions... millions....

**Black on Jim's Flashback - Doc's Story**

**Lights Up on Jim's Flashback - Doc's Story Continuing**

Outside the hospital room, the Old Man is in a wheel chair. Chazz brings Doc unwillingly. Chazz moves away.

OLD MAN

How ya doin', Doc?

DOC

Hectic.

OLD MAN

This will just take a minute. Last night I said some things.

DOC

You were excited.

OLD MAN

Look, what I said... did anyone else overhear our little conversation?

DOC

I don't think so.

OLD MAN

You'd tell me, if anybody did.

DOC
Of course.

OLD MAN
You spent the night with me... in my room.

DOC
You asked me to.

OLD MAN
I tend to talk in my sleep... I'm old... feebleminded... did I say something?

DOC
I sedated you fairly heavily. You slept the whole night.

OLD MAN
Yeah, I felt rested. But you were gone when I woke up.

DOC
Your driver came in to relieve me. And another guy.

OLD MAN
Yeah, they told me. Listen, I want you to have this.
(takes Doc's hand)
If you know what's good for you, you'll forget all about last night.

DOC (V.O.)
Figured that...

**Black on Jim's Flashback - Doc's Story**

DOC (V.O.)
...was the best thing. Then he invited me and my girl up for dinner sometime. Just like that. How about dinner... you and your girl?

**End of ACT I**
**Scene Four**

**ACT I**
**Scene Five**

**Lights Up on Jim's Flashback - Continuing**

Jules' boat - Night. Doc finishes his story.

JULES
That's a hell of a story.

JIM
Hoffa and Kennedy? Come on... why not Marilyn?

Doc takes out a crisp one-thousand-dollar bill. He passes it around. The others pass it amongst themselves.

EDDIE
That real?

JULES
Very real. And he's got five million in his bedroom?

JIM
I've heard some bullshit stories --

CORRINE
-- And you've told most of them, Jim.

JIM
Hey.

JULES
You don't know his name?

DOC
No.

CORRINE
But the address --

JULES
-- Forget about it... it's a good story. Shit, it's after four. I'm hittin' the hay. Get the hell off my boat. All of ya. Baby, I need the car early. You mind dropping her off, Doc?

DOC
Not at all.
(leads Corrine away)

EDDIE
Thanks for the drinks. Later.

Eddie leaves behind Doc and Corrine.

JIM
That was interesting.

JULES
We're talkin' five million just sittin' there.

JIM
We're talkin' the mob. Doc's too smart for that. Hell, I'm too --

JULES
-- If I had the address... I could come up with something.

JIM
Ten says Doc never goes for it. We should stick with the medical stuff.

JULES
Screw that. One last score. All we need is Doc on the inside with one of these.

Jules holds up a bugging transmitter, watching Corrine and Doc.

JIM
With his girlfriend in the way? Come on --

JULES
-- Not his. Mine.

JIM
Corrine? And Doc? He'd still never go for it.

JULES
(watching Corrine and Doc in parking lot)
He'll go for it. If I know Corrine, he's goin' for it right now.

JIM
(sees the look on Jule's face)
You sicked her on him.

JULES
I don't have to like it.

**Black on Jim's Flashback**

**Lights Up on Jim's Flashback - Continuing**

Marina Parking Lot. Corrine walks with Doc to his car.

DOC
Maybe this isn't such a good idea, us being alone like this.

CORRINE
Why? I've been thinkin' a lot about us, Doc.

DOC
Because I've been thinking too much about us.

CORRINE
Say the word and I'll leave him.

DOC
Corrine....

CORRINE
(leans on him)
Say it.

DOC
Stop. You'll get us in trouble.

CORRINE
We could afford trouble. I could get away. You could take better care of your mom.

DOC
That's hitting below the belt.

CORRINE
Just get the address. Jules will work out the details. Please. For me. I need this.

DOC
We're not ripping off the old man. I'm not helping you.

CORRINE
Fine! I don't need your fucking help.

**Lights to Black on Jim's Flashback**

**Lights Up on Jim's Flashback - Continuing**

From boat, Jules and Jim watch Corrine march back up the dock.

JULES
Shit, he's not goin' for it.

JIM
Make her go down on me and I'll beat it out of him.

JULES
Shut up.

JIM
I'm serious.

JULES
So am I.

Corrine jumps on the boat and storms past them and into the cabin below, slamming the door.

JULES
I didn't tell you to get pissed off.

CORRINE (O.S.)
He won't help us.

JULES
Just do as I told you.

CORRINE
(comes back out)
Maybe he'll let you suck him off, Jules. Better yet, why not Jim, at least he might enjoy it.

JIM
Shit, for a million dollars, you bet I would.

JULES
Screw 'em, we'll do it another way.

**Black on Jim's Flashback**

**Lights Up on Jim's Flashback - Continuing**

Int. Henry Ford Hospital Emergency Reception Area . Doc stops Corrine from thumbing through files.

DOC
It's not in there.

CORRINE
Where's his file?

DOC
I put it in a safe place. I want to talk.

CORRINE
Just give me his file and get out of my face.

DOC
Corrine... let's talk, for a minute.

CORRINE
Only if you give me the file.

DOC
This thing, these people you're with, this is not good.

CORRINE
The old man is a killer... and deserves to get ripped off. Now give it or I start screaming.

DOC
If we go up there, to that house, and the money ends up missing, who do you think they'll come looking for? Us.

CORRINE
We don't do anything. We have dinner. The only time we'll leave the old man's sight is when I go powder my nose and text Jules. If they catch anybody, it'll be him.

DOC
There'll be alarms, armed men.

CORRINE
Jules knows that... he'll work it out. Just get us the address. Men want me, Doc. But you, you have me, just --

Corrine tries to kiss him, Doc holds her back.

DOC
-- It's not like that. It can't be.

CORRINE
But, Doc --

DOC
-- I mean it, Corrine... my mom's.... If we do this, it's for her. And I tell Donna about it.

CORRINE
Whatever. Offer still stands

**Black on Jim's Flashback**

**Lights Up on Present Day - Continuing**

The Coffee Can - Night. Chazz and Leon sip their caps. Jim has ice to his eye.

JIM
Can you believe that, the momma's boy? She might've been bullshittin' me, but I doubt it knowin' him. We needed Doc in on this was all I cared. Why didn't matter. What's a little head among five million dollar partners? But you should've seen the look on Jules' face when she lied and told him it was the first time she liked it. And how big Doc was. She liked to mess with Jules, you know. Am I boring you guys?

Chazz and Leon just look at him.

JIM
Anyway, at least I didn't have to.

Black on Present Day

**Lights Up on Jim's Flashback - Continuing**

Doc shows up at Jules' boat. Corrine gives him a hug. Jules watches. Jim and Eddie are drinking.

JULES
You got it?

DOC
I got it.

EDDIE
Five million.

JIM
If the old man ain't just some lunatic.

JULES
Shut up, both of ya. Get us some grub, Corrine.

CORRINE
What am I? The cabin girl?

JULES
Just get it. Don't give me a hard time.

CORRINE
(takes out her phone)
Chink, wop, or spic?

JULES
There's leftover cold cuts down below.

CORRINE
Then eat it, Jew Boy.

JULES
Who the hell do you think you are?

CORRINE
Someone who is perfectly capable of deciding what and who she wants to eat.

JULES
Ain't this a bitch?!

DOC
Can we get on with this?

JULES
Back off. Get down there.

CORRINE
I don't want your lousy leftovers, you cheap bastard. I want pizza.

Jules slaps her. Doc shoves Jules away From Corrine. Jules punches Doc in the face. Eddie and Jim try to keep them apart.

Finally, Doc kicks Jules' ass. Corrine goes to Doc, looking at his hands.

Jules is helped up by Eddie and Jim, he laughs it off, mouth is bleeding.

CORRINE
You could've hurt your hands.

JULES
What about my face?

CORRINE
Nothing could hurt that.

JULES
You want some more, kid?

DOC
If you hit her again, yeah.

JULES
I'll hit her whenever I want to... she's mine. Understand?

DOC
Perfectly.

Doc jumps off the boat. Jules motions Corrine to go after him.

JIM
What are you, crazy? We need Doc.

JULES
Order something. He'll be back.

EDDIE
What the hell is going on?

JULES
I don't mind her sucking on him when I tell her. I just don't like her braggin' about it. And I sure as hell don't like her wantin' more.

JIM
You are crazy... she was shammin' ya. Just to mess with your head for makin' her try. She even told me.

JULES
Order some pizza, goddamn it.

EDDIE
I don't know, them cold cuts sounded damn good to me.

Jules shoots him a look. Eddie picks up the phone.

**Black on Jim's Flashback**

**End of ACT I**
**Scene Five**

**ACT II**
**Scene One**

**Lights Up on Jim's Flashback - Continuing**

Outside Grounds of Old Man's house - Night. Jules comes back joining Corrine, Eddie, and Jim.

JIM (V.O.)
Anyway, we hiked up the hill and were huddled outside the Old Man's Mansion wall the very next day.

Jules takes out a drawing of the grounds. The house is in the middle. He's marked trees and gates. He shows it to them, with a pencil.

JULES
Either that tree or that tree, Eddie. Right now there's five of them prowling the grounds.

EDDIE
The one closest to the wall.

JULES
I want you to go out and practice with that rifle. Your life may depend upon it.

EDDIE
Don't worry... I know guns.

JULES
Jim, you wait out here for Eddie after you chain the gate. Stay put. If any shooting should start --

JIM
-- Shooting? You make it sound so romantic, Jules. Shooting. Like it's pulp fucking fiction. Think about it. Leaving our cars so far away. We could be dead walking up here like this. You, me, all of us. Just get in, rob him, get out. Don't be shootin' people, Eddie.

JULES
This isn't a kid's game. You want a play date, go to your mom's. Start walking. Now.
(stares Jim down)
The three of us will be wired in. Corrine, the patio has tables with ashtrays. You and Doc get out there, whatever the reason, go out. Take smokes. If there's an alarm, he'll shut it off.

CORRINE
What if he turns it back on?

JULES
Watch him. See how he does it. If you can't, just say so and I'll enter up here. There's a vent to the attic. Whatever you do, keep him out of the master bedroom.

CORRINE
That's it? What if you can't find the money?

JULES
I'll find it. Five million... shit I can smell it from here.

EDDIE
I can smell something.

The others look at Jim.

JIM
I'm nervous.

**Black on Jim's Flashback**

**Lights Up on Present Day - Continuing**

Int. The Coffee Can - Night. Jim is looking at his eye in the bar mirror.

LEON
Okay, fine, we can see wantin' the money. But what happened?

CHAZZ
Yeah, why hurt the old man? Why not just tie, gag, and run? You knew we were there. It don't make sense. Why start the shooting?

JIM
Things went just as Jules planned. The old man comes by about a month later and Corrine, as you know, goes with Doc up to the old man's house. Only, from what I heard, the old man swung a little fruity....

**Black on Present Day**

**Lights Up on Jim's Flashback Continuing**

Inside Old Man's Mansion Dinning Room - a month later - Night. The Old Man sits at the end of an elegant, candle-let table. Flanked by Doc and Corrine.

OLD MAN

Drink up.

DOC

I'm fine.

OLD MAN

Have some, I hate to waste this stuff. 1973 Zieregg Sauvignon Blanc. Grown right outside the Iron Curtain. So drink up. People died for this shit.

The Old Man passes the bottle to Corrine. She pours herself some and hands the bottle to Doc. Doc sets it on the table.

CORRINE

I'll drink his share. So where're you from?

OLD MAN

Back East.

CORRINE

New York, New Jersey?

OLD MAN

East of here. You two live together?

CORRINE

Yes.

DOC

No.

OLD MAN

(looks them over)

Which is it?

CORRINE

We have separate places. We just, you know --

OLD MAN

-- Hump a lot.

DOC

Ah --

OLD MAN
-- I would if I were you, kid. If you don't mind me sayin', Corrine, you're a very edible young lady.

CORRINE
I'm no lady.

OLD MAN
(gets up)
I was bein' polite. Why don't I show you the rest of the house? Leave the bottle, I got other stuff. This way.
(leads them out)

CORRINE
So, how long have you lived here?

OLD MAN
None of your business.

**Black on Dinning Room**

**Lights Up on Living Room**

Doc and Corrine following the Old Man. The place is old, dark, and full of things from around the world.

OLD MAN
Living room. Bar. Shit house over there, and there.

Doc and Corrine admire the Art.

DOC
A Picasso?

OLD MAN
A forgery. You want it, take it.

CORRINE
Mind if I smoke?

OLD MAN
Not in the house. I got lung issues.

DOC
There's an ashtray out here.
(reaches for the porch door)

OLD MAN
Hold on.

The Old Man goes over to a box on the sideboard. Opens it and takes out a remote. Points it at a spot on the wall.

OLD MAN
Helps me sleep at night. I'll be right back.

**Lights to Black on Living Room**

**Lights Up on Porch**

Doc and Corrine exchange looks as they go outside. They sit at a table. Doc takes her lighter and lights her cig.

CORRINE
You need to get into the box.

DOC
You'll have to distract him.

An armed O.S. MOOK walks past.

CORRINE
Nice night. Mook. This'll be easy.

OLD MAN
(exits house onto porch)
You done?

CORRINE
Almost.

OLD MAN
Put it out.

Corrine takes a deep drag, exhales. Snubs the cigarette out on the table.

Doc is stunned... but the Old Man just grins... locking eyes with Corrine.

OLD MAN
I got something for you.

The Old Man goes in. Followed by Corrine and Doc.

**Lights to Black on Porch**

**Lights Up on Living Room**

Doc shuts the porch door and the Old Man takes the remote and points it, tossing it on a side table.

OLD MAN

Make yourself at home, Doc. We'll be just a minute.

The Old Man takes Corrine's hand and leads her O.S. Leaving Doc in the living room... alone.

**Lights to Black in Living Room**

**Lights Up in Bar - Continuing**

Old Man pins Corrine against the bar.

OLD MAN

This is older than I am.

CORRINE

Then give me a stiff one.

OLD MAN

Can't... last time I nearly croaked.

CORRINE

Poor boy, maybe you could put me in your will.

OLD MAN

I want to watch you and Doc.

CORRINE

Do you? How bad?

OLD MAN

Five grand bad enough for you?

CORRINE

No.

OLD MAN

Seven-fifty. I ain't askin'.

CORRINE

Ten grand. Cash. Doc's a little shy.

OLD MAN

You're right, you're no lady.

CORRINE
Business person. Let me get my purse.
(stops him from groping her)
Doctor's orders.

OLD MAN
I'll just enjoy the show.

CORRINE.
Yes you will.

She walks away, lifts her dress to give a show. Glances over her shoulder.

**Black on Jim's Flashback**

**End of ACT II**
**Scene One**

**ACT II**
**Scene Two**

**Lights Up on Present Day - Continuing**

Int. The Coffee Can - Day. Chazz and Leon look at each other knowing all about the Old Man's sex exploits.

JIM
Ten grand just to do it. You imagine? I would've licked her dirty toes for a dime. But this lucky stiff was offered ten grand. All of us wired in. Jules man... damn. I'm gettin' a woody just tellin' ya. And the old man didn't even want in.

CHAZZ
He had to take pills. The last time scared him a little.

JIM
So you guys were friends of this --

LEON
-- It don't matter now. It's a diverse world.

JIM
Ain’t it. So I chained the gates...

**Black on Present Day**

**Lights Up on Jim's Flashback - Continuing**

Old Man's Bedroom - Night. Corrine leads Doc over to the bed. There's a bar on a roll cart beside a chair facing the bed.

DOC

This is...

Doc turns and Corrine pushes him on the bed. And gets on top of his chest. Her panties almost in his face.

DOC

... Corrine.

Corrine pins the Doc's arms over his head. Dress high on her hip, ass showing for the Old Man.

The Old Man positions himself in the strategically placed chair between a bar on a roll-cart and a small table, with lamp, and a gun.

CORRINE

He wants to watch us do it.

DOC

He --

CORRINE

-- Ten grand, Doc. Think of your school bills and your mom.

DOC

Not a --

CORRINE

-- Fifty-fifty. You'd like to do me right now wouldn't you, Doc?

OLD MAN

An investment in your future.

Corrine and Doc look eye to eye. They smile.

CORRINE

What do you say?

DOC

Mother won’t like this.

Corrine gives Doc a deep kiss, capping it off with a bite on his neck... and whispers...

CORRINE

Screw him. Make this creep get the money now.

(moves to the Old Man)

How about down stairs on the pool table?

OLD MAN

I like it here.

Doc sits up. Corrine takes the Old Man's drink. Gargles with it... spits it back in the glass, hands it back.

OLD MAN

You're a nasty bitch, aren't you?

CORRINE

You have no idea.

Corrine moves over to the bathroom door, slides in, looking at Doc as she enters. She closes the door.

OLD MAN

Let me see your dick.

DOC

Let me see your money.

The Old Man just smiles. He slowly gets up.

**Black on Old Man and Doc**

**Lights Up in Bathroom**.

Corrine turns on the water and sits on the toilet... PEES. She takes out her phone and calls Jules, wispering.

CORRINE

They're in the master bedroom. He wants to watch us. You heard him. I tried that. That's why I'm calling. He wants it up here. It's open and it's off. Think of something fast or enjoy the show.

**Black on Jim's Flashback**

**Lights Up on Present Day - Continuing**

Int. The Coffee Can. They're losing Jim to the pain. He's looking faint.

LEON

So, at this point they got to be thinking kill the old man or put on a show.

JIM

I don't know. I don't. Jules got in. The next thing... all hell is breaking loose.

CHAZZ

Yeah, we remember.

JIM

Then keep in mind, I'm still on the outside listening on the headset. But what I know....

**Black on Present Day**

**Lights Up on Jim's Flashback - Continuing**

Wall outside the Old Man's Mansion - Night. SHOOTING takes place inside and outside the Mansion. Jim crouches down alone the wall, fighting not to run. Two different GUNSHOTS explode just inside the wall.

JIM

Come on, Eddie.

Shooting stops. Eerie quiet.

JIM

He's dead... I told him... goddamnit. We're all dead now.

Eddie’s hands appear at the top of the wall. He barely makes it over, tumbling to the grown in front of Jim.

In shock at Eddie’s bloody face. Jim jumps to his feet and screams!

EDDIE

(crawls toward)

Take me with you. Please, Jim, don't leave me here.

Stumbling to his feet toward Jim... Jim falls down, scooting away on his butt.

JIM

You're a mess... you're dead... I told you... what am I suppose to do with you?

Eddie does his best to stay up. Stumbling toward Jim. He's a mess, blood everywhere.

EDDIE

Show some respect. Put me in the trunk, at least.

JIM

I got good shit in there.

EDDIE

I'd do it for you.

JIM

(getting back up)

Fine... stop, listen up, there's a few leathers and things... keep them away from your face.

EDDIE

Remember me....

Jim reluctantly helps Eddie O.S.

**Black on Jim's Flashback**

**End of ACT II**
**Scene Two**

**ACT II**
**Scene Three**

**Lights Up on Present Day - Continuing**

Int. The Coffee Can. Jim is noticeably disturbed by the retelling of Eddie. He's got real tears, and not from pain.

JIM

That's all I heard. We made it to my car and were at the boat when Jules and Corrine got back. Corrine went crying down below. Jules said Doc tried to kill him in the house. And that Doc shot the old man. Right in the head. Jules had to shoot Doc just to get out. But we had the money. That's all I cared about right then.

CHAZZ
Doc double-crossed everybody. Took all the money. We got a problem with that.

JIM
Look, I know, I had my doubts, too. But you should've seen her... Corrine was hysterical when they showed up. Something went wrong up in that room. Jules had to go down and slap some reality into her before cops crashed our party.

LEON
Get to the point before you croak on us.

JIM
We were just about to split the cash when Doc showed up. He denied everything. Had a gun... he took it all, the bastard took it all and Corrine with him. I know, it sucks, but it's how it went down. This much I do know.

**Black on Present Day**

**Lights Up on Jim's Flash Back - Continuing**

Jule's Boat/Dock - Later. Corrine and Doc back up the ramp. Jim and Jules exit the cabin. Jim points a gun. Jules pushes it down. They watch Doc and Corrine leave.

JULES
I'll see you again, Doc.

DOC
No you won't.

JIM
You just gonna let him go?

Jules looks at Jim, then the gun.

JULES
Throw it over.

Jules picks up his spare gas canister and starts splashing it around the deck.

JIM
What the hell?

JULES
Wipe and throw the gun over... as far as you can throw... and get out of here. I don't want to see your face around me again.

JIM
But we don't have the money.

JULES
With or without, that was the deal. Remember?

JIM
Yeah, but I thought --

JULES
-- You think too much, Jim. Throw the gun.

Jim wipes the gun and throws it out as far as he can.

JULES
Now beat it.

Jim jumps from the boat to the dock.

JIM
What am I gonna do? I got Eddie in the trunk.

JULES
You'll figure it out.

JIM
That's it? You're serious? Who's gonna fence my stuff?

JULES
I'm shutting down. Movin' on. I'd suggest you do likewise in case the old man's stories were true.

Jim thinks this over. It's a scary thought. He heads for the dock.

Jules grabs up a traveling bag and jumps off the boat. He lights his lighter and tosses it onto the boat. Before it BURST into flames.

**Black on Jim's Flashback**

**Lights Up on Present Day- Continuing**

Int. The Coffee Can, Jim really looks pissed. Still hurt from it all.

JIM
All them years we'd been together. I came that close to shootin' them all. If Jules hadn't've stopped me... I don't know... I don't like shootin'... but five million dollars... maybe I would've.
(sees their skeptical looks)
Back then... I'm a legit business man now.

CHAZZ
Yeah. So, where are they? Jules, Corrine?

JIM
Not a clue. I spent three years in prison for armed robbery shortly after, then two years on the street, living in my car. I didn't get no postcards. The bastards... you know what it's like bein' a punk in prison?

LEON
Not lately.

JIM
Guy like me? I ain't sat straight since. Yeah, if I had found Doc back then... and don't think I didn't look... maybe I'd'a killed him. I don't know for sure.

CHAZZ
So Doc got the five million.

JIM
Yeah. What did he do with all that?

LEON
Nothin'.

JIM
Jesus, this world stinks.

LEON
He was a gimp livin' in a dump, drivin' drunks home in a heap.

CHAZZ
A bum's bum.

JIM
I don't get it. Maybe he did give it to the church... or his mother.

LEON

We checked.

CHAZZ

So how do we go about finding the others?

JIM

Well, Eddie's dead... I know he ain't got it.

CHAZZ

Jules and Corrine.

JIM

Try the phone book.

Leon slams Jim's hand on the bar with the bat.

JIM

Okay, okay... shit, I was gonna tell. I went lookin' for them after I got out. Look what... I just had this counter done. But it was hopeless. They were gone. Then one night, while panhandling outside a liquor store, I spotted her popping out of a Porsche. So I followed her, wasn't easy in my piece of crap... but man, she was livin' good.

Chazz and Leon look at each other.

**Black on Present Day**

**Lights Up on Jim's Flashback - Continuing**

Outside Corrine's Home - Night. Jim makes sure no one is watching and knocks on the door.

Corrine opens it, expecting to sign for something. Has a marker.

CORRINE

Thanks for...

She's startled to see a bum. She slams the door. Jim sticks his foot in it.

JIM

Ah, shit, come on, I'm not gonna hurt ya.

CORRINE

I've got a gun and I know how to use it, mister.

JIM
Relax, Corrine, or whoever you're callin' your beautiful self these days. It's me, Jim Stock.

Corrine, thinking of how to handle this before slowly opening the door. She's got a big ROCK on her finger. She looks Jim over. He looks her over.

CORRINE
What do you want?

JIM
Well, the bimbo's all grown up.

CORRINE
You look like shit, Jim.

JIM
Thank you. Seen Jules?

CORRINE
Not in years. What do you want?

JIM
What do you think I want?

CORRINE
Look, my husband will be home any moment.

JIM
Any moment. I'd love to meet him. Tell him some stories.

CORRINE
I don't have any money here.

JIM
I just need a few hundred bucks to get back on my feet.

CORRINE
I told you....

JIM
I'll wait.

CORRINE
If I gave you a few hundred you'll just be back.

JIM
I might... who knows? I missed ya, you know... I fantasized about your ass the whole time I was takin' it up there in prison. You think I'm kiddin'?

CORRINE
What are your plans?

JIM
I was thinkin' of, you know, opening up my own place... some place far from here.

CORRINE
How far?

JIM
Depends on you.

CORRINE
Hold still.
(writes on his forehead)
It's my pager. Call it in one hour. I'll call my business manager and --

JIM
-- You got a husband and a business manager? What are you now, a movie starlet?

Corrine just looks at him.

JIM
I always thought you'd be good in porn. Jules had some footage of you. Talk about --

CORRINE
-- You through with the bullshit, Jim? I'm offering you a second life.

JIM
I'm sorry. I'm... shit I need off these streets. I want to stay clean, Corrine. You don't know... things ain't been... my mind ain't... I get this face... Eddie's face, it... remember...? He... shit.... I ain't eatin' right... this ain't right, you and me livin' so different like this.
(sees she doesn't care)
.... How much life we talkin'?

CORRINE
If I help you, I don't ever want to see your face again. You hear me? One hour. Call it. Minute after that, I change the number.

Jim lowers his face and nods that he understands. He looks back up at her. Corrine closes the door in his face.

**Black on Jim's Flashback**

**Lights Up on Present Day- Continuing**

Int. The Coffee Can - Night. Leon is making another round of caps. He gives one to Chazz. They carefully sprinkle chocolate and whipped cream on them.

JIM
His face... I live everyday with that shattered face.

CHAZZ
They stick with you sometimes.

LEON
So she set you up? Not a bad place.

JIM
Thanks, beats climbing in windows. She started a bank account in my name not far from here where I can only borrow upon it. For business purposes. "The Coffee Can"... come to me while I was in. Ten grand.

CHAZZ
And you never saw her again.

JIM
I swear. It was the deal. She gave me a life. I'd let her live hers. I'm a changed man. A tad demented perhaps. But I'm definitely not goin' back to that other life. Ever.

LEON
So where do you suppose she got the ten grand?

JIM
She was married.

CHAZZ
Where is she?

JIM
Please, don't hurt her.

CHAZZ
We just want a chance to ask her the same questions.

LEON
Maybe you'd like to run this place by Braille?

JIM
Okay, okay.
(tries to write, but can't)
Shit... you write it. 1583 Lake View, Grose Point, just off the Lake. Last I knew, that's where she was. I don't even know if it was her place.

Leon writes it down. They down their caps. Chazz closes the sports page.

Jim stands there with the ice rag over his eye. Hoping they don't kill him.

They leave him alone, going out the front door.

Relieved, Jim waits to make sure they're not coming back before reaching for a counter phone, but stops after dialing, with a startled look in his good eye! Phone ringing on the other end.

JIM

Don't... DON'T!

Jim covers up, but the bat smashes on his head. Jim slides to the floor as Corrine picks up on the other end.

CORRINE (V.O.)

Hello, hello?

The phone cord is slowly pulled upwards.

JIM

Coming... for... you.

CORRINE (V.O.)

Who is this? Who..? Jim? Who, Jim?

DONNA

(steps into the light with the phone)

Me, bitch.

**Black on Present Day**

**End of ACT II**
**Scene Three**

**ACT II**
**Scene Four**

**Lights Up on Present Day - Continuing**

Int. Corrine's Home - Bedroom - Night. Corrine hurriedly packs more things. She's half dressed. She's going away. Far away.

CORRINE
Take that one. Give me a minute. I got one more suitcase to get. And I need to....

Corrine is startled to find Chazz and Leon at the bedroom door. She makes a run for the patio but Leon tackles her on the bed.

CHAZZ
Here's the story. You tell us everything or we play tag team. Jail house rules.

CORRINE
I don't know what you want.

CHAZZ
We want to know where the money is.

CORRINE
What money?

LEON
He's gonna like this.

CORRINE
Look, I don't know who you guys are. Or what you want.

CHAZZ
We want to know who ended up with our money.

CORRINE
Are you sure you have the right person?

LEON
You want top or bottom?

CHAZZ
You know me. I'm a butt man.

Leon flips Corrine over.

CHAZZ
Where's Jules?

CORRINE
Okay, okay, I haven't seen him in years. I'm telling you the truth.

CHAZZ
How do we get a hold of him?

CORRINE
His office number is in my book. Over there. On the table.

CHAZZ
Who's got the money?

CORRINE
I don't.

CHAZZ
Who does?

CORRINE
Doc does. You've got to know he was smarter than all of us. Played us for fools.

LEON
Last we knew he had no brains.

CORRINE
I thought Doc was a sweet guy. I wanted to run away with him. I would have, too. But he went crazy.

CHAZZ
Humor us if we sound confused.

CORRINE
Doc was... he had this whole other side.

**Black on Present Day**

**Lights Up on Corrine's Flashback**

Yacht Club Parking Lot - Night. Corrine walks Doc back to his car after the fight.

DOC
What did you tell him?

CORRINE
I... ah... I told him a little fib... about us... to get him mad.

DOC
Jesus... he throws a punch.

CORRINE
I don't want you sticking up for me again. Do you hear me? I can fend for myself.

DOC
You're welcome.

CORRINE
I don't want to see you hurt.

DOC
When this is over... so are you and Jules. I'll see to it.

CORRINE
Come on... I was mad at him... I had it coming.

DOC
You can't let that bastard.... Am I bleeding?

CORRINE
Careful what you say, Doc. I like you. At times I might even think I'm falling for you.

DOC
Corrine...

CORRINE
When this is over. If you still want this. We'll talk. But you see how he is. Jules will never just let me go on my own. We'll have to give him what he wants.

DOC
Leave Jules to me.

**Black on Corrine and Doc**

**Lights Up on Corrine's Flashback - Continuing**

Int. The OLD MAN'S bathroom - Night. Corrine stands at the door, listening.

CHAZZ (V.O.)
So, tell us about you and Jules that night?

CORRINE (V.O.)
Things got a little twisted... and Doc... the old man was, you know....

The bathroom light clicks off. O.S. Gun SHOT.

DOC (O.S)
I told you not to touch it!

**Lights Up in Old Man's Bedroom**

Corrine quietly opens the bathroom door.

Light from the windows illuminates the room.

Doc is standing there in the shadows with the Old Man's gun. His pants undone. The ten grand in his other hand. A crazy look in his eye.

The Old Man is in the chair... dying.

Suddenly Jules enters from the hall.

Doc, startled, fires at him. Missing. Corrine screams!

Jules fires back. Hitting Doc in the side. Doc flops down on the bed.

Jules closes the door, locks it, and moves over to Doc. Holds him down. Taking the ten grand.

JULES
(yelling at Corrine)
Stack shit in front of the door. Do it, now!

Corrine, in near panic, stacks things against the door.

Meanwhile... shooting starts from outside around the grounds.

Jules grabs Doc off the bed and throws him on the floor.

JULES
Where's the rest of the money?

Doc doesn't answer.

Someone tries to open the bedroom door. Pounding.

Jules steps on Doc's stomach.

JULES
Where... and I'll let you live.

DOC
Against the wall, beside the bed.

Jules looks down, seeing Doc reach for the Old Man's gun. Jules kicks it under the bed.

Jules moves to the wall and opens a floor plate behind the bed and pulls out a funny old child's suitcase. He opens it on the bed. The suitcase is full of thousand dollar bills. Puts the ten grand in it.

Corrine moves to Doc, goes to her knees.

CORRINE
Jesus, Doc. Why?

Doc opens his mouth to answer but Jules pulls Corrine up and over to the balcony door.

Someone starts shooting at the lock on the bedroom door. Doc begins to crawl under the bed for his gun.

Jules opens the upstairs balcony door and pulls Corrine out. Corrine takes one last look at Doc.

Jules fires at the bedroom door. The shooting stops.

**Black on Corrine's Flashback**

**Lights Up on Corrine's Flashback- Continuing**

Jule's Boat and dock - Night

CORRINE (V.O.)
We made it to our car. I was screaming at Jules for shooting Doc. He punched me out. Next thing I remember we were getting out of the car at the boat.

Jules and Corrine reach the boat. Corrine is not cooperating. So Jules pushes her onto the boat. Then takes her into the cabin and slams the door on her, turning on Jim. Corrine is screaming inside.

Jim covers his ears.

JIM

Is that it?

JULES

Where's Eddie?

JIM

Eddie's in my trunk. Dead. I'm not sure about Doc. You've got to do something about her.

Jules drops the suitcase and heads for the cabin.

JIM

What happened in there?

JULES

The son-of-a-bitch started shooting at us?

JIM

The old man?

JULES

Doc!

Jim stands there in disbelief as Jules goes into the cabin.

O.S. Jules goes inside the boat's cabin and grabs a pillow and puts it over her face.

Jim covers his ears, hoping up and down.

But she continues to scream O.S. under the pillow.

JULES (O.S.)

You gonna shut up, huh, you gonna shut up? You gonna shut the hell up?!

Suddenly Jim goes to the door and grabs Jules from behind and pulls him off Corrine and on deck into the light.

Jules turns and stage and punches Jim in the face, knocking him down.

Corrine staggers out gasps for air, throws the pillow at Jules.

CORRINE

You prick!

JIM

What the hell's the matter with you, Jules? You could've killed her.

JULES

Shut up, the both of ya. Get the money and bring it down here.

Jim turns to get the money but stops. And is backed away by a gun to his chest.

Doc, who also has the suitcase of money, and bleeding bad, follows the gun across the deck.

DOC

Back off, Jim. Drop the gun.

Jim drops the gun. Doc kicks it away.

JIM

You're, you're, you're... Jesus... you're a walkin' dead man.

DOC

Yeah, your friends did me good?

(points the gun)

Get up, Corrine, get up!

CORRINE

But I didn't --

DOC

-- Pretty slick, hitting the breaker switch, Jules. Me and the old man playing show and tell. Don't look surprised, Jim. They weren't planning on splitting any of this.

Jim looks from Jules to Corrine and back.

Corrine turns around. Doc grabs her by the hair.

DOC
We're backing out of here. And you're making sure I get to some friends who can fix me.
(backs Corrine off the boat)
Sit down, both of you. Hold hands. I said hold hands.

Jim takes Jules' hand. Jules gives Jim a look, but doesn't sit down.

DOC
That's how I want to remember you two sweet guys. Thanks for trying to screw me.

Doc backs out with Corrine. Doc stumbles against the boat. He's still bleeding badly. Corrine is crying.

CORRINE
You've got to listen to me.

DOC
I'm not interested in any more of your bullshit.

CORRINE
Me? You killed the old man. You fired at Jules. You're acting crazy.

DOC
I trusted you. And you left me there to die.
(stops, puts gun to her head)

CORRINE
I didn't want to leave you. What was I to do? I don't know what happened... but it wasn't me. You shot first.

DOC
Shut up.

Doc backhands her with the gun. She covers her head with her arms and goes to her knees.

CORRINE
Please, Doc, don't do this... leave Jules his share or he'll find you.

DOC
Put your arms down. Get up. We got to get to my car.

CORRINE
You've got it all wrong. I'll help. Whatever you say. But Jules will find you... anyone connected to you. Me, your mom, Donna... you can't....

Headlights flash on them. Doc stops. He lowers the gun to her heart so the driver can't see it.

DOC

Eyes forward, let's go. You make a move to run and I swear to God I'll splatter what little heart you have left all over this parking lot.

Doc coughs and drops to his knees. Corrine knees him in the face and runs O.S.

Doc picks himself up, turning the gun on Jules and Jim. He looks crazed.

He tries to stand up straight, but can't. He just manages to drag himself and the suitcase off the dock and out of the light.

**Black on Corrine's Flashback**

**Lights Up on Present Day - Continuing**

Corrine's Bedroom - Night. Corrine wipes her eyes blows her nose into the sheet.

CORRINE

That was the last time I saw Doc. I called Jules to let him know where I was. He wanted nothing to do with me. Called me a bunch of horrible names.

CHAZZ

But you got his office number.

CORRINE

A year or so ago my husband and I ran across Jules at a luncheon. He gave me his card. We weren't alone, so the subject never came up.

CHAZZ

And you never called him.

CORRINE

Once. Jim looked me up. He needed money. So I called Jules. I couldn't ask my husband for that kind of money. Jules gave it to me to help Jim start a business. I'm married now to a very nice man. I made a few mistakes. But the past is the past. After what I've gone through, I'll do whatever you want. Just don't touch me.

CHAZZ
What we want is the money? If Doc had it, what did he do with it?

CORRINE
I don't know.

CHAZZ
Then let's call Jules. Tell him Doc has found you, and he's coming here.

Leon gets off her. She pulls the sheet to cover herself. Chazz hands her the phone. She dials from the book.

CHAZZ
Tell him to come here right now.

CORRINE
Mr. Steadmen please. Jules? It's Corrine. He's found me. Doc! He's coming here, right now. Any minute. I don't know what he wants. My car's in the shop! Please come, right now. Help me.

CHAZZ
Steadmen now, huh. You're pretty good at this hysterical game.

Chazz looks at the phone book. Something's not right.

**Black on Present Day**

**Lights Up on Present Day - Corrine's House - Living Room/Bedroom-Continuing**

Jules enters the unlock door - Night

JULES
Corrine?
(reaches inside his coat)
Corrine, you here?

Chazz steps out of the dark... puts a gun to Jules. He pats him down. Taking a gun from Jules' coat.

CHAZZ
Inside, Mr. Steadmen.

JULES
What's this?

CHAZZ
You'll remember soon enough.

Chazz brings Jules into the house. Corrine is there with Leon. She's still got only the bed sheet on over being half dressed.

LEON
Been a while since you had to watch another man with her, huh, Jules.

JULES
What's this all about?

CHAZZ
We want our money.

JULES
What money?

Leon grabs Corrine by the throat. Kisses her.

CHAZZ
When we're done with your wife, Jules, we start on you.

JULES
My wife?

Leon throws Corrine down on the couch.

CHAZZ
There's no business phone number in Corrine's book, Jules. Just your cell. And why? Because the clothes in the closet are yours. And though we didn't know what you looked like, we do now.
(picks up a framed picture)

JULES
Okay, fine, we still know each other. But we're not married. There's photos of other men there. Look around, you can see I don't live here.

Chazz punches Jules right in the face. Jules slides down the wall near a closet.

CHAZZ
I already owe you one for a hole in my chest, so don't push it.

JULES
All right, okay, I'll give you what's left.

Jules crawls over to the closet and opens it. There's a FLOOR SAFE in it. Jules opens it. Chazz pushes him aside with his foot and reaches in, pulling out the Old Man's childish suitcase.

JULES
There's over a million dollars there. Just leave us alone.

LEON
Isn't that romantic? All this time these two love-turds stuck together.

JULES
So you found the others.

CHAZZ
Yeah, we found them.

JULES
Then it was you in the house.

CHAZZ
We're friends of the old man. You took our money.

JULES
Your money?

LEON
Never said we were good friends.

CHAZZ
Waited for the old man to croak naturally. You beat us to it.

JULES
You're right, we did rip him off. But it was her. She starting shooting.

CORRINE
He's lying, I swear.

CHAZZ
Are we suppose to give a shit?

JULES
I'm not a killer. She killed the old man. She shot Doc, too. You see she's got the money.

CORRINE
What the hell are you doing?

JULES
She hid a gun somewhere. Maybe planning to cut us all out... I don't know... then Doc showed up thinking I shot him. But she fixed him real good. She told me herself.

**Black on Present Day**

**End of ACT II**
**Scene Four**

**ACT II**
**Scene Five**

**Lights Up on Jules' Flashback**

Marina darkened parking lot. Corrine holds two guns on Doc. His and hers.

CORRINE
Don't look at me, just step over to the ditch.

DOC
Back there, I was... I thought --

CORRINE
-- What? That I loved you? Maybe I do. A little. Not enough to split five million.

DOC
(picks up the money)
Take the money, just get me to my friend's --

CORRINE
-- Your friend a mortician?

DOC
Jesus, am I stupid.

CORRINE
I'll send flowers to your mom.

Corrine shoots Doc in the right shoulder and he falls O.S. Corrine keeps shooting, pissed as hell... both guns.

**Black on Jules' Flashback**

**Lights Up on Corrine's House - Living Room/Bedroom - Continuing**

Corrine is pissed. The guys don't care. Leon pushes her down on the couch again.

JULES

I caught up with her at my condo. Or she might've cut me out, too.

CORRINE

You stinking liar.

CHAZZ

Look, it's been a long day. We got what we came for. So, why don't you move over close to her.

JULES

You don't need to kill us... please understand --

CHAZZ

-- Understand this.

Chazz takes a swipe with his gun at Jules' head.

But Jules rebounds from the blow by grabbing Chazz's gun hand, twisting it around. And shoots...

... Leon with it. Leon, in shock, falls back, pinning Corrine to the couch.

Chazz smacks Jules in the face with the suitcase. Pulls the gun away, and shoots Jules in the forehead. He turns around just in time to find...

... Corrine still under Leon, but now struggling to take aim with Leon's gun.

Chazz fires first, but the bullet sinks into Leon.

Corrine is finally able to pull the trigger.

Chazz gets it good, just under the suitcase full of money. He goes down. Slowly drowning in his own blood.

Corrine pushes Leon off her to the floor and gets up. His blood soaking the sheet.

She peals the sheet away, standing there triumphantly... gun in hand. The Gangster slayer.

CORRINE
Men are so stupid.

Corrine runs into her bedroom, pulling on clothes quickly, grabbing up her last suitcase.

Something stops her when it goes thump in the living room. Corrine moves back into the living room, counting the bodies.

She quickly moves to get the money. But it's not there.

She turns to find... Donna standing at the front door... with the gun Chazz had taken from Jules. And the child's suitcase full of money.

DONNA
Hello, bitch.

CORRINE
Please. Jules made me do everything.

DONNA
Yeah, yeah, I heard the whole tear-jerker. Pardon me if I don't weep for any of you crumbs.

CORRINE
There's enough money in there for the both of us.

DONNA
There's not enough money in the world for the both of us. So here's taxes plus late charges on the money you already spent.

She shoots Corrine. Corrine doesn't go down.

DONNA
And this is for all the debt I got from Doc's unfinished med school.

Shoots Corrine again. She still refused to go down.

DONNA
This is for ruining my life.

Shoots her again. Corrine drops to her knees.

DONNA
And this is for being a sick, double-crossing cunt.

Donna shoots her again. Corrine drops to the floor. Dead. Donna stands right over her.

DONNA
And this... is for the memories.

Shoots her again. Feeling vindicated. She turns to leave and finds Doc standing at the door. He's unarmed and crippled from his old wounds. Donna is shocked.

But not as much as Doc by what he's just witnessed.

DONNA
Doc?

DOC
I'm too late....

DONNA
Try five stinkin' years too late.

DOC
I'm so sorry.

DONNA
You should be. You won't spend any of this.

DOC
No, Donna. For you. Because of the pain I caused you over that money.

DONNA
Pain? Look at you. I don't give a shit about the pain, you ass. Money, Doc. The fucking money you promised me from all this would've been nice.

DOC
I know... I never got any.

DONNA
Of course, you were a fool then, and you're a bigger fool now.

Donna points the gun at Doc. But instead, a gun goes off from behind her. The bullets rips right through Donna and... hits the wall behind Doc.

Chazz's gun drops from his hand. He lies there barely alive.

Donna is in disbelief.. Blood oozes out of her mouth as she drops to her knees. Still trying to pull the trigger, and gets off a wild shot... shattering things.

Doc moves to catch her... even before the gun clicks empty. He holds her up from the floor, sinking to her knees to gently hold her. Blood dripping through his fingers.

DOC

Donna, I'm so sorry. I was wrong. I made a mistake. I trusted her. I should've listened to you. I'm not the person I used to be. Don't die... you can keep the money... Donna...?

Donna's eyes open back up. Her head is over Doc's shoulder, her mouth near his ear. She can barely talk.

Donna coughs up more blood.

DONNA

Doc... Oh, God... Doc....

DOC

Yes, baby, I'm here.

DONNA

Go fuck whoever you think you've become.

Donna dies in his arms. Doc holds her.

A gurgling laugh comes from Chazz.

SIRENS fill the air as Doc sets her gently down, looks around, finding who pulled the trigger.

Chazz lies there looking up at Doc, let's go of his gun.

CHAZZ

What a bitch.

Doc, squats on his knees, empty. This is all his fault. And he knows it.

CHAZZ

How did I mess up?

DOC

You killed the wrong sinner. Last Christmas I gave Bullhead dress shoes I didn't wear anymore. I was in the alley waiting when he went through my car.

Doc crawls over to see if he can stop the bleeding.

DOC

Bull collected cans and bottles. You gave him a ten spot to tell you where I worked. I watched you toss my place. Found Donna's letter missing from the car. I tailed you... then Donna showed up at The Coffee Can. She hurt Jim real bad. You guys didn't help. I tried to save him... but he didn't make it. I should've known... I messed up... I killed you all, didn't I.

CHAZZ

Nah, none of us is any good. But you, you meant well... did it for her and your ma. Put your medical future on the line for them.

DOC

It doesn't make it right.

CHAZZ

A lot of gray matter in-between right and stupid, Doc. You had to know I'd come someday.

DOC

The evil one. Yeah... I knew. I knew someone would.

Doc can't stop the bleeding. Chazz stops him.

CHAZZ

I took a lot'a shit back east. You gettin' out of that house.

DOC

There was a vent. They were paying attention to you. Can I get --

CHAZZ

-- just take the money, Doc. Nobody from my world knows we're here or why. Take this.

(hands Doc Donna's letter)

DOC
(takes out Donna's picture, reacts to the memory of her)
This money, his life, did the old man really kill all those people? Kennedy, Hoffa?

CHAZZ
Somebody did.

DOC
I didn't kill the old man.

CHAZZ
Yeah, I'll tell him that when I see him
(dies)

Doc sits there. The money beside him. What's left of the Old Man's five million.

He looks around, deciding what's best. He looks at Leon, Donna, and Corrine.

The SIRENS are rushing at him.

He gets up.

Picks up the money and walks out.

Stage Lights Up With Cop flashing lights through the door and window!

**Lights to Black**

**CURTAIN**

# WHEN THE RIGHT MAN FINDS YOU

**A Neo-Noir Thriller Tragedy Stage Play**

**(based on the screenplay)**

**by**

*Karl J. Niemiec*

(inspired by a true story)

**CHARACTERS:**

**MARLEY GRAYSON:** Mid-30s. Graceful, classy, a real head turner and new owner of the local weekly newspaper.

**BO FOSTER:** Late-30s. Tall, manly, muscular, very talented woodcraftsmen. Owns the arts and craft store Bo & Arrow.

**ARROW:** Bo's older dog. (Note: Play can be done with or without).

**SALVADOR TURK:** 30s. A gangly strange and dangerously secretive, mentally challenged man. Bo's childhood friend.

**SAM NEGAHBAN:** 50s. An owner of a construction company.

**HOOMAN ZANIB:** 20s. Simple minded construction laborer.

**JACLYN:** 40s A plump, bossy newspaper office employee.

**JUDY:** 50s. An overly thin woman, newspaper advertising, and possibly Jaclyn's lover.

**MATTHEW JONES:** 70s. A cranky old newspaper printer.

**SHERIFF BROWN:** 50s. Small town cop.

**SETTING:** Int. and Ext. of the dimly lit McClure House - in Northville, Michigan. It's a majestic, Turn-of-the-Century Victorian home, with magnificent potential for the right amount of care and money. However, rundown, with overgrown trees and shrubs and vacant for many years. The horn like chimneys make it spooky and haunted looking at best. There are grand front double doors that open onto a once beautiful foyer a with splendid staircase and a landing on the second floor that leads to bedrooms.

It sets on a slight hill above a small deep lake toward S.R, and overlooks downtown Northville further S.R. Also S.R., a gazebo needing attention extends from a wraparound veranda; with a small family fenced-in grave yard just beyond it.

A dock and a brick boathouse that runs along the lake. No one in their right mind would live there as is, let alone remodel it.

However, this play can be done with minimal sets and props where the vision of the home, grounds, dock, and lake can be left up to the production or simple envisioned on the playbill so the audience can use their imagination throughout the play.

**TIME:**

Present day/night, Summer to following Spring.

Note on use of ancient wood as part of the plot: From TED Case Studies - Lake Superior Sunken Logs.

In Checaumegon Bay, Wisconsin, on Lake Superior, the Superior Lumber Company is involved in the recovery of millions of sunken logs 60 feet below the bay's surface. Because the logs have existed for approximately 100 years at large depths and in very cold water, they have been preserved almost to perfection. Most of the old slow growth wood at the bottom of the bay was clearcut in the late 1800s from areas in Canada, Minnesota, Wisconsin and Michigan, and were floated downstream to ports in lake Superior to be loaded onto ships for transport. During the 1930s, most of the northern Midwest old growth forest was deforested, and the large timber corporations had begun to leave the areas, along with all the timber at the bottom of Lake Superior. Today, treasure hunters like Scott Mitchen are involved in an effort to raise approximately one million logs to the surface of Lake Superior to be processed and sold to furniture makers, architects, contractors, instrument makers at high prices.

**CASE NUMBER:** 421 - CASE MNEMONIC: SUNKWOOD
**CASE NAME:** SUNKEN WOOD USE

**ACTS - SCENES:**

**ACT I - Scene One** - Night: Ext. Front of McClure House
**ACT I - Scene Two** - Morning: Ext. McClure House
**ACT I - Scene Three** - Late afternoon: McClure Gazebo

**ACT II - Scene One** - Day: McClure Yard
**ACT II - Scene Two** - Next morning: McClure House
**ACT II - Scene Three** - Hours later: McClure House
**ACT II - Scene Four** - Spring Day: McClure Gazebo

**At Rise:**

**ACT I**

**Scene One**

**Lights up on Ext./Int. McClure House**

Darkly lit sidewalk in front of McClure House - Night.

MARLEY GRAYSON enters the property from the street, heading toward the McClure House front gates. Her arms full of the blueprints and a briefcase. She can't see a thing. She steps onto the sidewalk and right into BO FOSTER checking a text while jogging. SMACK! Blueprints and cell phones flying. Bouncing back, but just before she loses her footing - BO recovers enough to stop her fall. Pulling her quickly, though inadvertently into his arms.

BO

Good evening.

MARLEY

Oh, my goodness. I'm so, so...

(right in his face)

Good evening. Ah....

BO

Bo Foster.

MARLEY

Marley Grayson.

BO

Right. From down the hall.

MARLEY

You live in my apartment building? Yes, with the beautiful dog.

He lets her go. Starts picking up the phone and blueprints. He's pissed about something and she's not sure why.

BO

Yes, Arrow. You're the News Paper Publisher?

MARLEY

Yes, that's me. I guess. Have we met?

BO hands her the blueprints and phone.

BO

In a way. I was the person secretly bidding against you on McClure House.

MARLEY

(checks her phone)

That was you?

BO

Yes. And you have no idea how you've broken my heart. I've had my eye on this house for over a year.

MARLEY

I'm truly sorry... Mr. Foster.

BO

Now I've got my eye on you. And it's Bo.

MARLEY gets everything back in her arms.

MARLEY

Thank you, Bo. I think.

BO

Do you run?

MARLEY

Only when chased.

BO

Good. Nice to have finally met.

BO jogs away. MARLEY stands there. She looks at the dark house then over at the town and lake. And heads up the front steps.

Int. McClure House Grand Foyer. MARLEY enters. She turns on a standing work light.

EVERYONE

CONGRATULATIONS!

MARLEY drops everything and lets out a BLOOD CURDLING SCREAM!

Only to find those standing there are as shocked by MARLEY'S reaction as she was at finding them there.

MATTHEW
Told you surprising her in the dark was a harebrain idea. Nearly killed the poor woman.

MARLEY tries her best to compose herself. She looks over at her employees JACLYN, JUDY, and MATTHEW JONES.

The girls smile back warmly. MATTHEW frowns. SAM NEGAHBAN, in workmen's clothing, is doing his best not to laugh. SHERIFF BROWN, holds a tray of cookies. He's stupefied by MARLEY'S reaction.

MARLEY
You guys. It's dark and spooky... Jaclyn, Judy, don't... thank you, you shouldn't have. I mean it.

MATTHEW
Don't blame us. Your new neighbors insisted. Just tell the Sheriff you'll vote for him... and he'll go home.

JUDY
Oh, Matthew, don't --

MATTHEW
-- Got a paper to put out. Now drink your coffees and eat your cookies and let's go back across the street and work.

JACLYN
You old coot, hush up.

SHERIFF
(steps forward)
Mr. Jones is right, Jaclyn. Marley, we just wanted to stop by and give you these. Cookies. We are the official McClure Park welcoming committee.

SHERIFF hands MARLEY the cookies. MARLEY looks but finds no place to put them.

SHERIFF
Home baked by the misses. Welcome to Northville.

MATTHEW
She's lived here five weeks, Sheriff. Owns the paper now, remember?

SHERIFF
Yes, and as of this morning the proud owner of McClure House. And founder of McClure Park.

MARLEY
Thank you, all. I'm more than surprised. Horrified even comes to mind.

MATTHEW
Old rotten dump.

SHERIFF
And it will once-again be a grand manor. I'm sure.

MATTHEW
Better hope her other grandma dies.

JACLYN
Matthew, now you hush. Marley's semi-retired.

JUDY brings MARLEY a wrapped ream of paper with a big red bow.

JUDY
For your first Great American Novel. Written in your soon to be restored dream home. McClure House.

MATTHEW
Be a haunted house story. Things movin' around up in here all the time. Scarin' the heck out of simple folks. Me workin' nights, I see things up here all the time.

JUDY joins JACLYN, boxing MATTHEW in.

JACLYN
Her contract with you says she can't fire you. There's nothing in it that says we can't hurt you. Now go on about your work, old-man - and let Marley enjoy her special day. Go on.

JACLYN
He's harmless.

JUDY
You just gotta kick-start the old coot's smile on special occasions. Come on, Sheriff, we'll buy you a beer.

SHERIFF
Now you're talking. Good night, Marley. Reach out if you need anything.

MARLEY
I'm sure I will. Thanks for the cookies. Good night, everyone.

JUDY and JACLYN usher MATTHEW out the door.

MARLEY
Sam, you have no idea how relieved I am to finally make this decision.

SAM
Don't worry, Miss Grayson. We'll get started on the final blueprints in the morning. Why don't we meet up here. Say, tenish, and we'll go over a few things I think you should know.

MARLEY
Know? Is there something wrong?

SAM
Oh, no. Nothing out of the ordinary. It's just that there was a fire up in the rafters back in 1950. They walled in some of it. And I think we should open it up and take a good long look at them chimneys behind it.

MARLEY looks out the window. Reacts to who she sees.

MARLEY
I see. I want to keep them of course. All eight fireplaces. I'm thinking of having new mantels carved. Each with a different material. Here, take these, it'll save me a trip.

SAM
(picking up blueprints)
There's a lot of critters living up in that area. And I can guarantee you they've made themselves at home. But don't fret. Happens in these old places sittin' empty for so long.

MARLEY
(walks him to the door)
Tomorrow then, Sam.

SAM
Can I tell you a little secret?

MARLEY
If it won't cost me a thing.

SAM
Been praying to get my hands on the McClure House for ten years. Dreaming of leaving it to my family. Even if this is as close as I get, you've made me a happy man today.
(looks out the window)
The gentleman you're keeping an eye on out that window, is from the craft shop. Don't think he'da used me. Looks like he'da done it himself. I sure would've.

MARLEY
Well then, Sam. Just keep that in mind when I start changing my mind on what I want.

SAM
Don't worry. Ask around town. I'll look after you.

MARLEY looks out the window for Bo again. JACLYN comes back in. Big smirk on her face. MARLEY gives her a look.

JACLYN
Just checked the office messages. You had a phone call.

MARLEY
Must've been a good one.

JACLYN
Didn't leave a name but said the chase is on. And it starts at the McClure House gazebo with Starbucks when you're done screaming in here.

MARLEY
Did he?

JACLYN
He sounded handsome.

MARLEY
Looks even better. But I think he's mad at me.

JACLYN
You go, girl. Take your phone - case I need you.

MARLEY
I'll meet you at the office in an hour.
(pats her purse)

JACLYN
(goes out the door)
Run don't walk, girl. If that was Bo Foster, I'm liable to beat you to him.

JACLYN leaves as MARLEY catches her reflection in a broken mirror. She fixes her hair, before picking up the cookies and leaving out a side door leading to the gazebo, veranda, and docks.

BO sips STARBUCKS. A cup sits waiting for MARLEY. Arrow, his dog, is there at his feet. With them is a gangly man, SALVADOR TURK.

MARLEY
Wasn't expecting you so soon.

BO
My business partner wanted to meet you. He's leaving for home soon.

MARLEY
(sticks out her hand)
How do you do? I'm Marley Grayson.

SALVADOR
(doesn't shake her hand)
Hello.

MARLEY
Cookie?

SALVADOR
No.

BO
Thanks. Counter person told me what you add to your coffee.

MARLEY
Thank you. Sheriff Brown brought these. So, where's home?

BO
Actually Wisconsin. Went to Cranbrook. Art school. Then Auto Design.

MARLEY
I'm sorry, you lost me. You're from Wisconsin?

BO
Salvador and I both are.

MARLEY looks at SALVADOR. Trying to draw him into the conversation.

SALVADOR
Rhinelander.

MARLEY
Primarily a resort area. Isn't it?

SALVADOR
No.

A moment of uncomfortable silence.

BO
I came to Michigan to design cars. Salvador still lives there. Keeps an eye on Pop and some investments for me.

MARLEY is very aware that SALVADOR isn't thrilled that she is there.

MARLEY

Oh, so Cranbrook is here in Michigan. Right, right. Off Woodward.

BO

Take it you're not from around here, either.

MARLEY

Me? No. No, I'm not.

SALVADOR

Where are you from?

BO

Sal.

MARLEY

Traveled mostly. From paper to paper. You know, living out of a briefcase. So how did you get from auto design to working with wood, again?

BO

Sal and I grew up in the woods. Owned chain saws.

MARLEY

You do chain saw carving?

BO

Some of it. A lot of hand carved furniture. But some power tools as needed.

MARLEY

Really, I was told you had an Arts and Craft Store, Bo and Arrow's. No one mentioned hand-carved furniture.

BO

It's been our little secret.

BO indicates SALVADOR. MARLEY smiles at him but SALVADOR still isn't pleasant.

SALVADOR

Games about to start.

MARLEY

Right. Well, I really should go.

BO

Hold on, Marley. Sal, I'll catch up to you.

SALVADOR

But --

BO

-- Ten minutes.

Uncomfortable good-byes. MARLEY gets up. SALVADOR gets up and leaves.

BO

It's okay. Please sit, I want to show you something.

BO takes out a folder of photographs and hands it to MARLEY.

BO

These are from ancient logs pulled from the Great Lakes. Some sank in the late 1800s. There's millions of them in Checaumegon Bay. At the bottom of Lake Superior, close to where Sal and I grew up. Arrow, the boss here, watches over my work.

MARLEY

(before opening the folder)

Good job, Arrow. So, are we talking driftwood?

BO

Oh, no. That's the magic of it. The water's depths at near freezing temperatures preserved the wood.

MARLEY

Really? How'd you find out about this?

BO

Two guys are pulling them out of the lake. Salvador knows them. Hooked me up.

MARLEY

Ah, the middleman.

BO

(stops her from opening folder)

Now, hold on. What you're about to view is some of the most precious wood left on earth. The kind of wood they made the very first Stradivarius from. Incredible wood grains. A freak phenomena of nature. Like it was fresh cut just yesterday. We understand? This is between us.

MARLEY looks to see if he's being serious.

MARLEY

Before we go any further. Are you still mad at me?

BO
I'm not angry. I'm heartbroken. Take a look. I think you'll understand.

MARLEY opens the folder, stunned at first then quickly with growing excitement goes through them.

MARLEY
Are these...? Wow, Bo. Where did you get these designs?

BO
Library, town hall, private photos. Your newspaper. Some of the original built-ins still exist, but damaged. Others stolen. Once Sal found the wood, I decided to start fresh. Most of the originals were made right here in the very woodshop I now own. With turn of the Century craftsmen tools.

MARLEY studies the pictures closer. She's amazed. Almost afraid of the lunacy of it all.

MARLEY
So, you're the one who's been stomping around up there in the dark scaring people. But... you didn't even own the house.

BO
Yes, measuring. Until you came along I had no real competition. Other than Sam Negahban. But I heard he'd given up.

MARLEY
I had no idea.

BO
It was a surprise. I know how it looks. Relax. I had to act now. Most of this wood took over two hundred years to grow. It's no longer growing on Earth. Clearcut before 1930.

He pulls out a piece of chestnut wood from his pocket - sanded smooth.

MARLEY
Old growth. The denser the forest. The lesser the light. The slower the growth.

BO
Right. Time made this grain a jewel. From my own backyard. Believe me, this American chestnut is on a limited offer. It was once called the credal to grave species because of what was made from it.

He extends it for her to feel. They hold the piece of wood together.

BO

They think there’s maybe four alive today that lived before the blight fungus from the original four billion in America. It wasn’t even native to Wisconsin and not introduced until 1885. You don't even want to know what this goes for on the open market.

MARLEY

Actually, I would.

(looks at Bo. Another moment)

BO

And you'd be wrong in thinking that.

MARLEY

Really? And what am I thinking?

BO

Mid-life crisis. I'm not even forty yet.

MARLEY

I just bought a bankrupt Weekly Newspaper. And a rundown haunted house, overlooking a bottomless lake, in a town I never heard of three months ago. You want to talk about life crisis? Or do we just want to call it a big whatever.

BO

Ok, big whatevers.

MARLEY

I must have some of this.

BO

I was hoping you'd say that.

He moves over to a canvas covering something against the house wall. And pulls it off. MARLEY is in disbelief. Before her is a magnificent hand carved maple wood fireplace mantel.

MARLEY

Oh, my goodness, Bo. I want this. If you sell this to anyone else, I'll murder you in broad daylight.

MARLEY moves to it, touching the finish.

BO

Relax. It’s maple. I carved it for McClure House. An exact replica of the one that burnt in 1950.

MARLEY turns to him. "Who is this man?".

BO
I told you. You broke my heart. I love this old place. It talks to me. It's waited all this time for me to find her.

MARLEY
Well, I'll have to find a way to mend it, won't I.

Arrow jumps up on her.

BO
I guess we start with a walk.

They move up on the verandah overlooking the backyard. Arrow runs O.S. FLUSHING DUCKS.

MARLEY
You should've let everyone know what you were up to.

BO
Are you kidding? I can't let local artists know I have this kind of raw wood in my warehouse. Once they started bidding on it, I couldn't afford not to sell it. They'd hate me for hoarding so much of it.

MARLEY
Oh, come on. Are you serious?

BO
Yes. Think about what was made from just this maple during the 17th and 18th centuries. The Stradivarius' back, ribs, and neck for starters. The long list goes on from there. Seriously, if craftsmen who repair instruments knew I was making mantels, built in chairs, molding, and steps out of this ancient wood, for this old house, without owning it, they'd string me up in that tree. Not even the people selling Sal this wood know what I'm doing with it. Or that I’m involved. So, when I couldn't get Northville to commit to a practical or sane alternative, I decided to open my shop and wait them out. Hide what I was doing and build the furniture while stockpiling the wood.

MARLEY
Do you have enough to finish.

BO
Almost, I'm waiting on the last of the staircase. They haven't found it yet. But it's sure to be down there.

MARLEY
Of course I knew there were other bids. If it makes you feel better, I cheated.

BO
(walks Arrow into the yard)
Really. It all came down to a probate hearing for me. I couldn't get past the McClure family estate being left to the City of Northville. Under the stipulation of finding someone to restore the house. And properly move the four McClure graves.

MARLEY
(following)
Enter your first mistake. Where there's a legal will. There's a legal way.

BO
Enter a lot of mistakes. Not all by the living. The plan was to parcel off the land and bring in two similar homes. And use the one land sale to finish the remodel. But the City kept dragging their feet. And the neighbors kept voting no on parceling the land.

MARLEY
I don't blame them. Look at all this. Why change it?

BO
The place would've nearly paid for itself. The grand plan. Then you came along. With working capital, buying up that old paper, and an acceptable solution to burst my bubble.

They stop at a picket gate. BO pushes it. A long eerie squeak. Inside is a graveyard with four names carved on a large headstones with one space open. The McClures.

MARLEY
I see. I guess it came down to a matter of how one interpreted the idea of the McClure graves being here.

BO
How did you get around the original McClure will? How did you get these McClures buried with the rest? If all the adjoining plots were taken? And don't tell me you bought them up. Because people other than me tried that. People with real influence and money.

MARLEY
Simple. It hasn't been announced yet. So button the lip until my paper's out tomorrow. My first big exclusive.

BO
You better not make me look stupid.

MARLEY
I agreed to leave the graves here.

BO
But... come on, you're kidding, right?

MARLEY
There's nothing in the will stating that the bodies had to be removed. It just said if they were moved.

BO
Then they'd have to be put with the rest of the family. But if they're not.... Damn.

MARLEY
I gave this one-acre back to the City.

BO
Isn't that considered bribery in some states? Collusion or something at least downright sneaky?

MARLEY
It's called we're dedicating a small park. McClure Park.

BO
But this land is zoned to build. Think what could be... there's enough room to.... Right, you wouldn't want someone to build. If it's a city park. They never will. Anyone wanting to move a house in --
(remembers something, checks phone)

MARLEY
-- Can move it somewhere else.

BO
But you still cheated, right.

MARLEY
Yes. I cheated by digging into the archives of Northville Weekly. Which used to be a daily paper. And found who first owned the adjoining lots to the McClure land.

They start across the five acres after Arrow.

BO
All family members from what I've read. I cheated too. The news paper's archives are available in the library.

MARLEY
Of course.

BO
Damn. Have I said that? I just didn't get out of them what you did. A park. All this land was built upon by one McClure family member or another. Why not a park?

MARLEY
Right. Unofficially this area is referred to as --

BO
-- McClure Park. Damn. I could've grabbed the house and sat on it.

MARLEY
So, I merely suggested to my neighbors that we make it official. Partially funded by me.

BO
Merely. Sweet, Marley. Just leave the graves. Even the empty one for the missing child. Maybe put in a family statue in his honor. Why didn't we think of that, Arrow? I could've carved the statue of the boy myself. Damn, I made myself look stupid.

MARLEY
And I got myself a nice tax write-off to help me rebuild, too. And a basket of cookies from my new happy neighbors for keeping our adjoining land as is.

BO
Go ahead, rub it in. So, you're foxy and smart. I've got both my eyes on you now, sister. And Arrow does, too.

MARLEY'S phone RINGS. She looks at the number but doesn't answer it. BO isn't happy about losing the house. She senses it.

MARLEY
I'm sorry, Bo. Walk me back. You have to catch up with Salvador, don't you.

BO
Yeah, I better.

**End of ACT I**

**Scene I**

**ACT I**

**Scene Two**

**Lights Up on Ext. Int. McClure House**

Front of McClure House - Morning. MARLEY has stopped BO from jogging again. This time on purpose.

MARLEY
Okay, honestly. Which do you like?

BO
Give me a break, Marley. I'm cooling down already.

MARLEY
Come on, run in place. Just tell me. Which one?

SALVADOR walks up. BO and MARLEY stop.

MARLEY
Oh, good morning, Salvador. I thought you were leaving town.

SALVADOR
I didn't.

MARLEY
How was the game?

SALVADOR
We lost.
(gives BO a look)

BO
Take Arrow home first, will ya? He's down by the lake.
(whistles)

SALVADOR leaves.

BO
We're still waiting for wood. Okay, first off, which room?

MARLEY
Oh. I thought I told you, the foyer.

BO
Still? Then neither.

MARLEY
Come on. This pattern is perfect.

BO

Look, you've got the grand-staircase splashing down. Railings at the top, bending both ways. Twelve inch posts. Both stain and paint. As is, it's okay. But what I had in mind is something intricately carved. Dark and grainy. A focal point. Close to what was there originally but with better grain. Any kind of pattern beyond crown molding would only distract or clutter. Don't forget there'll be furniture, drapes, flowers, and paintings.

MARLEY

Flowers?

BO

Yeah, someone's bound to buy you some - someday.

BO whistles for Arrow. But Arrows gone.

MARLEY

He's with --

BO

-- Oh yeah. Have fun. I'll be over in a few minutes.

MARLEY

Thanks.

BO

Go put your tennis shoes on.

MARLEY

I'll go up and down the stairs a few times while I wait for you.

Bo smiles at MARLEY and jogs off. MARLEY retreats into the house.

In the daylight, McClure House - Foyer is a shambles from remodel, damaged walls, stripped, floors.

But in the middle of it all. Under the hammer pounding from upstairs, on an exquisitely handcrafted round pedestal table is a great big bouquet of wild flowers. MARLEY, joined by SAM look it over.

SAM

I have no idea how it got here. It was there when we got in. Damn fine work.

MARLEY

Have you met Bo Foster? Have you been in his Craft Shop?

SAM
No. But I've heard rumors about his work. Been wantin' to stop in. Tried once. No one seemed to be in.

MARLEY
Would you mind taking a minute to look at something? I want to introduce you. And show off the mantel he carved.

SAM
Now? He's a fairly private man.

MARLEY
Please? He's on his way. I just spoke to him. He's got drawings and photos I want you to look at.

SAM
Fine.
(yells up the stairs)
Hooman, I'm taking a break.

Pounding stops and HOOMAN ZANIB comes to the top of the steps. He might not be all there.

HOOMAN
Okay, but I want to show you something before you leave.

SAM
Can it wait? I'm not going anywhere.

HOOMAN
Sure it can wait. Whole house can wait. It's me that can't wait.

MARLEY looks concerned.

SAM
We'll be right up. Give us a minute.

BO
(enters with Arrow)
Good, you're here.

MARLEY
Thank you for the flowers.

BO looks over and sees the table and flowers.

BO
What's this doing here?

MARLEY
Don't even pretend you didn't have Salvador drop it off.

BO

You're welcome.

(sticks his hand out )

Hi, what the rude woman meant to say was, I'm Bo Foster.

SAM

Sam Negahban. Those for me.

BO

Sworn to secrecy. Right?

SAM

May I drown in the lake.

BO hands SAM a stack of drawings.

MARLEY

Don't say stuff like that, Sam.

BO

What? Sounds about right to me.

SAM looks over a drawing of a grand staircase. He can't believe it.

SAM

You could do this?

BO

Yeah, I had planned to - anyway. No time for it now.

MARLEY

He's just mad at me for outsmarting him.

SAM

Don't feel bad. None of us come up with it either. A park. I kicked myself real hard when I heard how simple it was.

BO

Actually it's the gloating that's got my jogging knickers in a knot.

SAM

It's a hell of a staircase. How much of the wood you got?

BO

Banisters and railings. Planning to go with something else on the steps. Hadn't decided.

SAM

You two figure it out. It's something to think about though. That's for sure if it looks anything like this table.

MARLEY

How can we not do it? Bo, please?

BO
I've got my shop, plus plans. I have to find a way to move all this stuff I've been holding on to. Before I move on.

SAM
Well, consider it. We won't need you right away. So you got time. But the mantel outside she wants. You can just leave it there?

MARLEY
I'll have a check in the morning.

BO
That's fine. I guess.

MARLEY
Thank you, Bo. We've been invited upstairs. Want to come.

SAM sticks his hand out. BO shakes it. MARLEY and SAM start to climb the staircase.

BO
I'm good. We can talk later.

BO turns to look at the work needed done. He wants this house. Now she's after his woodwork.

SALVADOR steps into the darkened window. BO doesn't see him yet.

MARLEY pops her head back at the top of the stairs. Startling BO.

MARLEY
Thanks for the flowers. And the table. I owe you dinner.

BO
Careful, or I'll take you up on that.

They look at each other for a moment. Sparks. MARLEY smiles and leaves. Arrow WOOFS.

BO
Yeah, woof is right.

BO looks over as SALVADOR, talking through window.

SALVADOR
I'm heading down to the railyard.

BO
Thanks, Sal. Pick me up about five pounds of these.

Bo tosses SALVADOR a small nail.

SALVADOR
You gave her the table?

BO
It's flawed. They sent it back.

SALVADOR
Yeah, sure.

BO
She's all right, Sal. Just go lightly.

SALVADOR
It's just... you know, not what we planned.

**Black on Bo and Salvador**

**Lights Up on Second Floor Landing**

SAM and MARLEY stand in the hall off the landing - Moments Later. SAM is mulling over the photos and sketches from Bo's folder.

MARLEY
Come on, you're killing me. What do you think?

SAM
He carved all that furniture for this house? Without even owning it first?

MARLEY
Yes. But what do you think?

SAM
I think the question is: What does his shrink think?

MARLEY
Sam. That's not neighborly.

SAM
Are you aware of how much money he has tied up in that wood?

MARLEY
So, he's a little eccentric.

SAM
Marley, I'm eccentric. You're eccentric. That's just nuts.

MARLEY
The house sat empty for years. Please, Sam. He can sell the work anywhere.

SAM
The house is weird enough as it is. Now this guy... and that odd friend of his... but okay, you're the boss.

MARLEY
What about his work? He's extraordinary, isn't he.

SAM
I think it's the most beautiful work I've ever seen. But it's not gonna fit your budget. And the blueprints. We'd have to redraw the whole front of the house.

MARLEY
But you can do it?

SAM
Yeah, I can do it. If I have his help. He's got a good eye.

The pounding from the master bedroom stops and HOOMAN sticks his head out of the door.

HOOMAN
You got time now?

SAM and MARLEY follow him down the hall.

SAM
The paint is fine, Hooman.

MARLEY
Is there something wrong with the paint?

HOOMAN
It's what's behind the paint you need to see.

SAM and MARLEY stop and look into a large hole.

An old CHEST sits covered in cobwebs. With a heavy chain lying on the floor. There's an ancient lock broken open. The lid's up.

MARLEY
Oh, my goodness, is that?

SAM
I'll be damned. It's a little boy.

HOOMAN
Called the Sheriff when you didn't come up. I couldn't figure why this wall was here. So I opened it. Looks like it was to hide fire damage.

SHERIFF (O.S.)
Nobody touch anything.

SHERIFF walks up from behind them.

SAM
Christ, Sheriff.

SHERIFF
Sorry, came up the service stairs. Who found him?

HOOMAN
I did. Broke open the wall and there he was.

MARLEY
Is this the missing boy?

SHERIFF
My guess he's Terrence McClure Junior. Disappeared June twelfth, 1919. Note said he'd run off because they euthanized his pony. Guess he didn't.

MARLEY
What do we do?

SHERIFF
Nothing we can do. Not a single family member alive. Except bury him out back with the others. Sam, why don't you send your boys home. I'll get someone official over here to clean up. That okay by you, Miss Grayson? Could have him cremated.

MARLEY
No, that's fine. It's the right thing to do.

SHERIFF
Seein' he's got space on a headstone down there, I guess. I'll check with the Mayor. Just nobody touch a thing. I'll be right back. I want to take some pictures.

HOOMAN
Maybe put my picture in your paper. Since I found it.

MARLEY
Sure, why not. You're a local hero. Solved the McClure mystery.

SAM looks out the window. BO and SALVADOR are still at the gazebo.

SAM
You guys got this?

SHERIFF
Let's keep this under wraps until we work this out. There ain't a next of kin.

SAM heads down the stairs as MARLEY goes to the window to look down at BO.

SAM
No worries.

MARLEY
I'll have Jaclyn write something up. This will be a big exclusive.

SHERIFF
Fine, but keep it simple. Until we find out what actually happened. Chances are he suffocated from the heat hiding up here. But who knows how he got in there, or why?

MARLEY keeps an eye down below. The Sheriff goes back down the service stairs. HOOMAN goes about putting away tools.

At the gazebo, BO looks up from a NEWSPAPER PHOTO. SALVADOR stops talking and puts the photo into his coat pocket as Sam approaches.

SAM
You got a minute?

BO
All day. Get back to me on that, Salvador. Just don't stress.

SALVADOR
Couple days, we'll know.
Sees SAM approaching

SAM
How ya doin'?

SALVADOR
Fine. Parkin' the truck, Bo.

SALVADOR continues past SAM. Looks back at BO. Walks off. SAM takes out the folder of photos.

BO
What's all the commotion, Sam?

SAM watches as SALVADOR leaves with Arrow.

SAM
Something the Sheriff's looking into about the McClure family. So, that's your guy? Seen him around town.

BO
Yeah. Middlemen. They make all the money.

SAM
How good are your blue prints on what you had planned for the McClure House?

BO
Pretty good. Did them up myself. Got them all on CAD.

SAM
Would you part with them if I were to buy up your furniture? Come work for me for awhile maybe?

BO
I don't think so, Sam.

SAM
Okay, well thanks. She wanted me to ask. I'll --

BO
-- Wait. She wants to buy up all my furniture?

SAM
Yep... and designs. Makes sense to use it all.

BO
And put it in McClure House? Just like that? Take my whole vision?

SAM
Well, Miss Grayson thinks --

BO glances over his shoulder at the veranda.

BO
What would she say if I just sold it all to a dealer?

MARLEY
(steps into view)
I'd say you were a big fat liar. What would you say to that?

BO

I'd say this is gonna cost you. And I'll need someone to mind the store.

MARLEY

I'd say we got a deal. If you promise to stop pouting over losing the house. Help us finish it before winter. And let me buy the furniture and woodwork on time.

BO

(looks at them)

I guess I'm in.

MARLEY

Good. You can tell him about the body we found now, Sam

BO

Body?

**End of Act I**
**Scene Two**

**ACT I**
**Scene Three**

**Lights Up on Ext./Int. McClure House**

MARLEY works on the Gazebo - Late Afternoon.

MARLEY

What do you think of this, Jaclyn?

JACLYN is on the phone, takes BO's photo from Marley.

JACLYN

I think we need to work in air condition, is what I think. But if you ask me, you got it bad, girl.

MARLEY

What? I'm doing a profile on a local artist and his work. Who just happens to be an amazing wood craftsman working on my home.

JACLYN

(hands photo back)

And I have Denial Washington's calendar on my bedroom wall because I still need to know what day it was back in 1999.

MARLEY

Give me a break.

JACLYN
Give me a break. You got "I will" written all over you.

MARLEY
I will what?

JACLYN
I will sleep with this man. You might as well face it. You're smitten. And there's a long hard road between "I will" and "I do". Remember that.

MARLEY
I don't know what you're talking --

JACLYN
(dials her phone)
-- Matthew, how many pages is the Foster profile?

MATTHEW (V.O.)
(speaker phone)
Four pages.

JACLYN
How many photos?

MATTHEW (V.O.)
Twelve.

JACLYN
Smitten, smitten, smiiiitten.

MARLEY
Matthew, cut the profile to two pages and one photo.

MATTHEW (V.O.)
I'm a printer, not an editor. You want it cut, you should actually speak to the man about something other than fabric or wood grain. There ain't a single bone in this article to help it walk to print. Lucky you got his last name right.

MARLEY
Okay, here he is now. Don't say a word. We're having dinner.

JACLYN
Uh-huh....

MARLEY
This proves nothing.

MARLEY grabs her pen and pad. JACLYN gets up and smiles at BO as she goes by, turning to give MARLEY a look. MARLEY shows her a clenched fist. BO sits down and looks after JACLYN.

BO
I see I'm not the only one with strange friends.

MARLEY
Jaclyn's not strange, just nosy, bossy, and a pain in the rump.

BO
Comes with the biz. Right?

MARLEY
I wouldn't know. So, you ready for your interview?

BO
No. Why don't we go to a movie instead. Double feature tonight. Bogie films.

MARLEY
Saw them already.

BO
Well, I guess I'm stuck. You want a beer?

MARLEY
You brought beer?

BO
No, I thought we'd go over and play darts at Bud's.

MARLEY
Drinking in bars makes me want to smoke again.

BO
Well, I can't think of anything else to avoid this. So give it your best shot, Lois.

MARLEY
Okay. Why Northville?

BO
Drove through a few times. Didn't want to move all the way back to Wisconsin. Sal had mentioned the wood. Found this house crying out for my help. Haunted me actually. Like it wanted that wood to save her. And a shop with the space I needed for my art shop.

MARLEY
And it came with the workshop?

BO
No, the adjoining workshop in back was just a lucky bonus. Kind've like it was meant to be. A simple matter of breaking through a wall. Why you?

MARLEY
I felt the same way about the house. Like it chose me to invest in it and give it new life.

BO
And I thought you just came here to break my heart and gloat about it once a week in your paper.

MARLEY
Stop. You're making me feel wicked.

BO
Don't. I'm just kidding... half. You did the honorable thing by buying the built ins. No regrets. But, why Northville? Where's home?

MARLEY
Home is here. My father was Air Force. Me being a journalist. You know. Hotel life. The paper was available. And I plan to write my Great American Novel in McClure House.

BO
Put down some roots in this old town?

MARLEY
Spent the last seven years looking after my grandmother. Living in one hotel after another. Maybe I do need roots. So here I am. Hey, I'm suppose to ask the questions.

BO
Is that dinner you owe me still available?

MARLEY
I offered you dinner?

BO
I have Arrow as a reliable witness.

MARLEY
How do you feel about delivery cooking?

BO
I thought I smelt something.

MARLEY
(reveals Chinese delivery)
Hope you don't mind. I took the liberty of ordering. I even picked it up.

BO
Looks like there's enough food here to feed five of us.

MARLEY
I got a variety pack. Just in case. Dig in.

They both open and serving themselves as they talk.

MARLEY
Any problem with red wine?
(glances up, then at her plate)

BO
Don't do that.

MARLEY
What?

BO
You're setting me up. I can see the sprockets churning behind your eyes.
(continues looking at her)

MARLEY
Stop. Talented, kind, handsome, hardworking - what's the downside? Thirty-five, single. Mamma's boy? Gay perhaps?

BO
It's that apparent? Darn.

MARLEY
You're not gay. Are you?

BO
Not last they told me. Why?

MARLEY
You know. The man and his dog thing. Flannel shirts. Work boots. Boyhood friend. Is that a real tape measure on your belt? Or are you just sizing me up for the kill?

BO
Oh, I see. The Village People thing. Only gay men are artistic and macho. The rest of us are just insensitive, out of shape, working-stiff bums.

MARLEY
Think about it. You have this Outer Craft-Shop, I'm a nice guy image. When just through magic shop curtains, there's this whole-other - obviously out of his mind - amazingly visionary guy. The real Bo Foster.

BO
Relax - I'm only out of my workshop. I'm a Craftsmen. You'll get use to it.

MARLEY
It's okay. I find them very handy these days. Like those shows on cable.

BO
Yeah, 'Bitter Hicks and Beer-Gardens'.

MARLEY
Okay, so you're not gay. Wise guy.

BO
Look who's talking, anyway. Beautiful. Somewhat mysterious.
(holds up one of the forks)
Refined taste. Overly intelligent. Seemingly wealthy. You know, just weird enough to be slightly out of butch camp.

MARLEY
Butch camp? I'm a little lady to the bone.

BO
Pantsuits? Dead giveaway. But most of all. You don't even have a dog. Not even a cat. At least I've a non-sexual excuse to be lonely.

MARLEY
Who said...? I can't think of a good reason to be lonely. What's yours?

BO
Just waiting for the right woman to find me. Who knows, maybe even the right man.

MARLEY
Smarty pants. You want dessert? Or a stroll through the park?

BO
Both.

MARLEY
I have it in the kitchen. Give me a minute.

MARLEY leaves. Bo picks up her fork and wraps it in his hanky, putting it into his pocket.

BO
I'm gonna stop by my place to grab a jacket. And, for the record, real men don't stroll.

MARLEY (O.S.)
Darn, I thought I had you.

**Lights to black.**

**<u>Lights Up McClour House - Later That Night.</u>**

Through the missing Master Bedroom bay window - Night. MARLEY and BO are making love, overlooking the town. They are wrapped in the cloth that covered the mantel Bo gave her. If this isn't true love, it's a good act. It's so perfect it hurts. Or at least SOUNDS like it does.

Down below in the gazebo, a gloved hand reaches out of the dark and picks up a half glass of wine from the table.

The gloved hand brings it up to SALVADOR TURK'S face as he steps into the light.

He sips. Thinking as he watches up at the window overlooking the street and town. SALVADOR can clearly see and hear MARLEY and BO making love up at the house. He's been cheated.

**<u>Lights to Black</u>**

**<u>Lights Up - Master Bedroom</u>**

Marley is asleep on the McClure House master bedroom floor - Early Morning. BO has gone. POUNDING on the missing door frame. Marley rolls over to find JACLYN staring down at her.

JACLYN
Girl, that must've been one in-depth interview.

MARLEY
Jaclyn, what are you talking about?

JACLYN
You don't know?

MARLEY
Of course I don't know. What time is it?

JACLYN
It's time you smelled the coffee. Let me show you something.

JACLYN comes into the room. And moves over to missing master bedroom window.

JACLYN
Tell me what you see and hear out there?

MARLEY
You falling, if you keep this up.

JACLYN
Take a saner look.

MARLEY
Jaclyn, I've got too much on my mind to --

JACLYN
-- Oh, the whole town knows what's on your mind, girl. Look for yourself.

Marley's looks out the window.

JACLYN
See or hear anything interesting?

Marley looks around below. Then slowly starts looking beyond at the buildings. She realizes that the window where they made love overlooks the town. It sinks in - in stages.

MARLEY
Oh, oohh... OOOHHH!

JACLYN
More like hoe, hhooe... HHHOOOE. Girl, I told you. You had it written all over your body.

MARLEY
Oh, my God!

JACLYN
You said that, girl. In fact, you said it many times from what I hear.

MARLEY
This is so.... Has he called?

JACLYN
Oh, he called. He's down in the gazebo. Waiting for a second cup of your hot-lovin'.

MARLEY
All right, fine. You were right, now go. Please? I need to run home and shower.

JACLYN
Uh-hummm. Press rolls in an hour. You got the edited pages?

MARLEY

Pages?

JACLYN

(goes out the door)

Girl, you got it so bad. You're late for work. Now you're the town slut. You better pull your act together. Judy had three calls from new advertisers wantin' to place web smut ads.

Marley wants to close the door but can't.

JACLYN

Bad, girl. Very bad. And what's worse? I'm so jealous I can't eat.

Marley turns slowly from the door. What has she done?

**Lights to Black**

**Lights Up on Gazebo - Continuing**

Gazebo - Morning. MARLEY exits McClure House and BO is waiting in the gazebo for her with Starbucks. BO has a confused look. Marley can't believe this. She moves over to BO and sits.

BO

What did you write about me in your paper?

MARLEY

Nothing yet. Look, Bo....

BO

I've had the most uninhibited conversation this morning. My shop is jumping. Fifteen people signed up for my art class.

MARLEY

That's not so bad --

BO

-- Half asked about nude models. The whole town acts like it got laid last night.

MARLEY

It did. Apparently, we were the center of attention... all night.

BO

Come again.

MARLEY

Oh, please.

BO

Marley.

MARLEY

Half the town watched and heard us enjoying Tiramisu.

BO

Tira...? Up in...? You're kidding?

MARLEY

I wish. I'm so sorry. I've got to go.

BO

Wait. Marley sit down. I've something I need to talk about.

MARLEY

Bo, can it wait? My paper is going to press without a main headline. And I apparently need to wash this slutty smirk off my face.

BO

No. Look, sit. Eventually our past will catch up with us.

MARLEY

What do you mean?

BO

We don't really know each other. But we know each other well enough. For example, I didn't exactly quit my auto design job --

MARLEY

-- Bo, I don't have to know this --

BO

-- Yes you do. And there's things I need to know about you as well. Just give me a minute. I was fired over an affair I had with a fellow employee.

MARLEY

Bo, really this isn't necessary. I --

BO

-- Yes it is. She wasn't exactly single. In fact, she was the boss' daughter-in-law. I want you to know. Because I want us to continue. And this might come back to haunt us.

MARLEY

The past is the past, Bo.

BO

I know this is sudden, but... I'm in love with you, Marley. From the moment I first ran into you. Truly. But I got her - she has my child. A two year-old boy. He doesn't know about me now. But someday, he might.

MARLEY hesitates, then breaks down and cries.

BO

Not exactly the response I was hoping for.

MARLEY

Bo. Please. I --

BO gets on his knees. Reveals a beautiful white gold diamond ring. MARLEY eyes light up.

BO

I made this from a stone my mother gave me. Knowing someday I would find the right woman for it. Marley, you are that woman. Let's start a family. Will you marry me?

She throws her arms around and kisses him.

**Lights to Black**

**End of ACT I**

## ACT II
## Scene One

**Lights Up on Int./Ext. McClure House**

Kitchen/Backyard/Gazebo - Day. The small reception after MARLEY and BO'S wedding. People we've met. Bo's on the phone in the kitchen.

BO

Look, Salvador. I know what I said. Yes. I don't want to know. No... Sal... damn it. Where are you? I told you I didn't want to know. Are you sure? I knew it. Damn you. Salvador, you can't tell anybody about this. Please. I've... Sal... we're married. I know what I said. Take the damn information and burn it, Sal. Sal? I mean it. Take -- Sal, don't do this. Don't do this to us. It was a mistake. Just throw the fork away. Do it now!

BO hangs up. Sam enters to get BO. BO is completely torn.

SAM

Everything okay?

BO

Huh? Oh. Yeah. I'm married to a beautiful, mysterious woman.

SAM

Come on, let me buy you an eye opening drink.

They exit the kitchen as JACLYN and JUDY enter.

JACLYN

It's a shame no one from their families could come and see all this.

JUDY

Jaclyn, you promised. We're her family now.

JACLYN

What? She looks so beautiful. It's a shame to have Sherriff Brown give her away. And Sam as his best man. It's... it's all I'm sayin'.

JUDY

Good.

MARLEY enters and the women stop talking.

MARLEY

What now, you two?

JUDY

Nothing.

MARLEY

Jaclyn?

JACLYN

I just... it's a shame that someone so beautiful - had to be given away by a toad like Sheriff Brown.

MARLEY

What's wrong with Sheriff Brown?

JUDY

She's just green with envy. Or just plain stupid.

MARLEY

Down, girls. Bo's father didn't want to make the trip.

JACLYN

Sure, his son gets married everyday to the slut of Northville. His best friend wasn't even here.

JUDY

Jaclyn.

JACLYN

Honey, if you don't know what's up with that boy's family. Then you need to ask some serious questions.

JUDY grabs JACLYN, marches her to the backdoor.

JUDY

Excuse us for one loud moment.

JACLYN

Let go of me, girl.

JUDY

(pushes JACLYN outside)

Shut up, or stay out of this room. She's been married but five minutes.

JACLYN

And known the man but two months.

MARLEY

Wait a minute. Stop right there. Judy, Jaclyn is right. Bo and I did rush into things. But it's okay. Bo's not on speaking terms with his father. It happens. This happens.

JACLYN

But... ouch.

MARLEY
I'm married to a wonderful talented man. We're in love. And we're renovating this house together. So shut-up and get out there and get drunk. Or you're both fired.

JUDY
(pushes JACLYN out the door)
Mouth.

JACLYN
We don't want to go there, girl.

But MARLEY stands thinking. GIGGLING. She turns to find a FLASH of movement but no one is there.

MARLEY
Hello? Hello?

Nothing. Then from behind her.

BO (O.S.)
Heeellooo.

MARLEY
My goodness, Bo! You scared the bajevees out of me.

BO
You look like you saw a ghost. What did you see?

MARLEY
Nothing, a flash maybe. But I heard giggling.

BO moves to her. Kisses her.

BO
He's just happy that he's finally buried with his family. Let's have a drink.

BO tries to lead her out but MARLEY stops.

BO
You okay?

MARLEY
I'm fine. It's just... I'm married.

BO
Me too. What a coincidence. Can I interest you in some married lovin'.

MARLEY
I'm very interested already.

GIGGLING comes from the same spot. They look at each other, then to the spot.

MARLEY and BO burst out of the house to the gazebo under a round of APPLAUSE and their FIRST DANCE. They compose themselves in each other's arms.

BO

We have a ghost.

MARLEY

You said you wanted a family.

They laugh, and dance away, as the small gathering joins them. JACLYN crosses her arm, eyeing them. JUDY pinches her playfully on the butt. JACLYN takes JUDY in her arms and they dance away.

In the upstairs window, SALVADOR is watching as down below the first dance takes place.

BO glances up to see him. SALVADOR lingers a moment, then steps back out of the window. BO's not happy about this.

**Lights to Black**

**Lights Up on Gazebo - Later**

MARLEY, BO, and ARROW at the end of wedding party. BO and MARLEY sit in the gazebo with a bottle of wine and cake. Arrow sleeps at BO'S feet.

MARLEY

Bo, I know we haven't talked much about this, so, if you don't mind, tell a little gazebo-tale about your childhood.

(BO cringes)

MARLEY

Don't if it's --

BO

No, it's.... My childhood was fine. Great even. But Pop disowned me when I decided not to go into the family business after high school. Paint store chain.

MARLEY
House paint? Colors. And I accused you of being gay.

BO
That's because I see rainbows whenever I'm with you.

MARLEY
Foster Paints. The chain? That's you?

BO
Yes, well, no it's my pop. A very large chain. I have stock though. So there's income. It angers him that I make money without helping him. Salvador still helps out once in awhile. Sal likes to watch the trains unload. And I think he still likes the fumes from the paint. He used to sniff it when he was a kid. You know getting high.

MARLEY
Not you?

BO
I had other ideas. I saw painted cars, not barns.

MARLEY
I see. I'm sorry about what this has done to Salvador.

BO
Yeah. I disappointed him.

MARLEY
Is he... he seems... so odd. Was it all the paint maybe?

BO
No. He's cool. His family were all odd. It's my own fault.

MARLEY
He got you all that wood.

BO
Yeah. There's not much he wouldn't do for me.

MARLEY
True friends are few and far between.

BO
Just before I went off to school he got into some trouble. Spent five years on probation. Couldn't leave the state. That was my fault, too.

MARLEY
He hurt someone?

BO
Kid came looking for me. Heard I'd been with his girl.

MARLEY
Were you?

BO
Yeah. Deserved to have my ass kicked many times. Sal broke the kid's jaw. Nearly put out one of his eyes. Wasn't for Pop saying the kid hit Sal first, he'da done real jail time. This house thing. He's a little upset by it. It's --

MARLEY
-- not your fault. There's other houses in this area.

BO
You got to understand Sal. He gets something stuck in his head. He fixates on that picture. He doesn't deal well with sudden changes. It upsets him.

MARLEY
He looks up to you. Like a big brother.

BO
Pop, kind'a was Sal's Pop, for the most part. We had a plan. Buy one house, and bring in two others. Sell one off. Live next to each other. Like when we were dumb kids. Before our families imploded, his family owned a lot of farmland. Lost it all to the bank after his pop took ill. We've talked about this old place a lot. It's what he sees his future is supposed to be. He never fully got over me leaving the store. Now this. It's tough on him.

MARLEY
It's your life. Salvador and your father must see that.

BO
We'll go see Pop one of these days. Maybe you'll tell him who I married.

MARLEY
Come here and make love to me. And I'll confess everything.

BO
Even the lesbian stuff?

MARLEY
Wise-guy.

BO
How about making some up? You know, college-gazebo stories.

MARLEY
Maybe they're real, maybe not.

BO
Big tease. Tell me about living with your granny.

MARLEY
My parents died in a plane crash. My father was a retired Four Star General. From there, Granny ran my private life pretty much. The insurance money just kept growing with investments. Granny was a smart business woman.

BO
You never bought a home before this one?

MARLEY
No need to. Granny liked the feel of hotels. And I was always on the move.

BO
So where are your parents buried?

MARLEY
Why?

BO
I don't know.

MARLEY
Their bodies were never found. Many plane victims aren't. You may have read about it. Can we change the subject?

BO
You brought it up.

MARLEY
I'm sorry. I harbor guilty feelings because they were on their way to see me. I bought them the tickets.

BO
Shit happens. I'm perfectly happy with the here and now. The past is behind us and tomorrow the Sun shall rise anew - a glorious day and shine upon our married life.

MARLEY reaches over for her wineglass.

MARLEY
To our future.

BO
And finishing the McClure House.

MARLEY
And our son, the ghost.

**Lights to Black**

**End of ACT II**
**Scene One**

**ACT II**
**Scene Two**

**Lights Up on McClure House - Gazebo/Foyer/Staircase**

BO working on the staircase - rainy Day. Thunder in the sky. Lightning.

MARLEY is on her laptop at the gazebo. She also has an unopened card.

BO looks up and sees her looking at the card. He recognizes it. He leaves the house and quickly crosses to the gazebo. He takes the card and looks it over. Trying to mask his concern. But doesn't open it.

MARLEY unpacks their lunch.

BO
On special days, Sal sends cards to us from my mother. She passed away unexpectedly some time ago.

MARLEY
Did I miss this part?

BO
Apparently. I'm not sure.

MARLEY
This is a strange custom among friends in Rhinelander?

BO
And not a topic Pop or I choose to speak about.

MARLEY
Or to me. Your family is getting to be quite colorful. Anyone else in the closet other than Sal and our little giggling friend? Sisters maybe?

BO
No. It's been years since he's done this. Back when I was let go. You know, so we don't forget her. Sal misses her.
(looks the card over)
It's a belated wedding card.

BO doesn't seem too happy about it. He doesn't offer it to MARLEY. But she holds out her hand anyway. He finally gives it to her.

MARLEY
(opens it with sharp letter opener)
She has very masculine handwriting. "She's someone special". Simple and nice. She thinks well of me.

BO
Good old Mom.

She hugs him. BO kisses her, and heads back to the house.

BO
I love you. No matter what.

MARLEY
I love you back. Regardless.

In both their eyes, there's something is bothering both of them.

MARLEY returns to the Internet. She's checking Wisconsin newspaper archives. Talking to herself.

MARLEY
Nothing. There's nothing here, Marley. The paint shops are there just like he said. He's got no criminal records that you can find. And he is whom he says he is. An ex-auto designer who was fired. This is foolish, you know. But --

JACLYN enters with her lunch.

JACLYN
-- But, you know what?

MARLEY
Jaclyn!

JACLYN
I coughed. Isn't it a little late to research the mystery lumberjack husband?

MARLEY
Was I talking out loud?

JACLYN
Yes, and if you're gonna continue. Talk louder so I don't strain myself tryin' to hear you. So, what did you find on mister, 'I don't know anything about'?

MARLEY
Nothing. Everything is how he said it was.

JACLYN
But your woman's intuition is burning a hole in your commonsense. Girl, I told you that. When the perfect man comes through that door, you better be on your knees in prayer. 'Cause he has done come again. The rest of 'em ain't nothin' but apple eaters.

MARLEY comes across something.

JACLYN
What is it?

MARLEY
Nothing. Now go back to work.

JACLYN
Don't come cryin' to me when you find he ain't the man he said he was.
(answers phone)
I got your lunch, Judy.

JUDY (V.O.)
Will you leave the woman alone?

JACLYN (O.S.)
Oh, girl, you don't want to go there with me today.

JUDY and JACLYN'S voices fade away.... But something is bothering MARLEY greatly. Her eyes well up with tears.

MARLEY
Unsolved disappearance? She's someone special.
(having a breakdown, answers her phone)
Hello. Oh, could you please text him on his phone? Yes. Of course. Just a minute.
(calling out)
Bo. Phone call on my cell for you.

Bo trots to the gazebo.

BO
What's the matter, Marley?

MARLEY
Nothing. Work related stress. It's for you. Did you give out my cell phone? Said he couldn't reach you on yours.

BO
Hello. Hey, Sal. Yes we were. No, I.... Come here, now.

MARLEY
What does he want?

BO
(looks sickened)
The wood.

MARLEY
Bo, what does he want? Bo --

BO
-- Don't worry. Sal's just.... He's coming here. I'll take care of it.

BO moves D.S. toward the street. SALVADOR waits for him there. They walk into the house.

A quick moment later, SAM sticks his head out an upstairs' window.

SAM
-- Marley, something's wrong. His guy's here with him. And Hooman took off a few seconds ago and didn't say where he was going. You see him send him back up here, pronto. I'll be back in about an hour. And you better get inside, storms coming quick.

MARLEY
Okay. I'll be right up.

MARLEY enters the house and stops at the bottom of the stairs as SAM comes out. He motions inside.

MARLEY enters the foyer to find BO has SALVADOR up against a wall.

BO
What did you tell them?!

The men stop when they see MARLEY. BO lets SAL go. And pushes him towards the stairs.

MARLEY is taken back by this violent side of BO.

SALVADOR comes down the half-finished stairs and past MARLEY without a word.

BO
Sorry, Marley, I --

MARLEY
-- What's going on? What's happening?

BO
Marley, it's nothing. The guy is putting a squeeze on me.

MARLEY
Why? What have you done?

BO comes down the stairs. He tries to take MARLEY in his arms but she backs off.

MARLEY
Bo. Tell me.

BO sits on the steps. He wants to tell her the truth, but can't. He looks at her, trying his best to sound truthful.

BO
The wood. He let someone outbid us. We won't get what we want until maybe spring or later.

MARLEY
This is about the wood?

BO
We're not just talking about any kind of wood. It's the only wood.

MARLEY
Bo, it doesn't matter if we --

MARLEY leads him out to the Gazebo.

BO
-- It does matter. There's no telling how long it'll take them to dredge up another log to match the grain we've started. If ever. People as far away as Japan are bidding on this wood. I'll have to start over if we don't get it.

MARLEY
For crying out loud. This damn wood. You're driving yourself crazy.

BO
It's not getting his house. I should've known.

MARLEY
It's only wood. And you're acting like a wanted man.

BO
Only wood? Marley, this is our home. This is our vision. I can't finish the stairs right without it. I can't take him to court or kick anyone's ass. We're screwed if he doesn't get us back in line for that wood.

MARLEY

Stop. Calm down. No court, no ass kicking. If we have to wait, we'll wait. Just stop this secrecy stuff. You're scaring me. Tell me everything is fine. That we're okay.

BO

Everything is fine. The "We're okay" I'm not so sure of until I make a few phone calls to see who got our wood. I told you, Sal's the middleman. Without him, there's no wood to finish this place. Not the way we want.

MARLEY unpacks the food, not letting BO see her face. He gets up and watches her for any sign that she knows what's going on.

MARLEY

Good. I can't believe you two are acting like this. I should write your mother and tell her what bad boys you are.

BO doesn't answer. MARLEY knows something. They're both in the game now. Bo takes his food inside as JACLYN enters the gazebo.

JACLYN

It's about time. You workin' out of this gazebo isn't conducive --

MARLEY

-- Not today, Jaclyn.

JACLYN

I need to have you sign off on these boutique articles before --

MARLEY

-- I'm serious.

JACLYN

Marley, the checks still haven't --

MARLEY

-- Do not make me yell at you --

JACLYN

-- And one of your workers just stopped by. I think he quit. He left something. I put it on your table there.

MARLEY

(picks up the sealed note)

Go back to your lunch.

JACLYN

But --

MARLEY

-- Now. And no more deadlines. I don't care if the paper is late once in a while.

JACLYN

It don't work that way. We got trucks comin' to pick up bundles in forty minutes.

MARLEY

They can wait.

JACLYN

Please, you're not talking --

MARLEY

-- Have Judy call the advertiser's bank and verify the amounts of the available funds in their accounts. This is not new ground here, Jaclyn.

JACLYN

Can you read these over at least?

(MARLEY looks at JACLYN)

JACLYN

Okay, fine. I'll have Matthew run these as is when I get back from lunch.

MARLEY

Not so hard, was it --

JACLYN

-- On lunch. It's your paper. I just work there.

MARLEY

Finally, we agree on something.

MARLEY opens the note with the sharp letter opener and reads. It's handwritten. Thunder sounds nearby, startling her.

HOOMAN (V.O.)

Meet me out back of the house, 11 A.M., sharp. Where I take my lunch, by the lake. Don't be late, your life depends on it. Just sit down on the end of the dock. I'll join you when I know you're alone. Hooman.

This is greatly disturbing to Marley.

JACLYN
Marley? What is it?

MARLEY
I'm not sure. It's nothing. He's quitting, like you said.

JACLYN
Girl, whatever it is, you best come clean. 'Cause you ain't a good liar. Or I'm gonna call the Sheriff.

MARLEY
Jaclyn, do you like working at my paper?

JACLYN
Not at the moment.

MARLEY
Give me the articles and get out of my gazebo.

JACLYN hands over the papers. MARLEY watches her go, checking her watch, and rushes out of the gazebo

**Light to Black**

**Lights Up - Continuing.**

Ext. Boathouse, Lake, and Dock - Day.

There's a brick boathouse with a dock running into the lake behind it.

MARLEY cautiously moves closer. There's a lunch bucket. Nothing else. So she sits down and waits as instructed. Going over the papers, checking them off.

Wind picks up, and the thunder rolls across the sky. It's creepy. She's looking around for someone, anyone. But no one comes out of hiding.

MARLEY
Hooman? Hello? Hooman?

Getting nothing but a DEAD ECHO back. MARLEY looks around seeing the dock runs beyond the boathouse out into the water. Realizing once on, there's only one dry way off. She looks down into the water.

She reacts to something O.S. in the water. She stands up in shock to get a better look. Moving further out along the dock. Uses the FLASHLIGHT on her car keychain to see into the water. Large thunder and lightning! She nearly falls in from the sudden thunder.

MARLEY
This isn't... NO! They can't.... Not now, oh please not now!

She stumbles back in shock. Papers go flying in the on coming storm. MARLEY realizes that she has put herself at risk. She's nearly at the end of the dock. She looks around in panic. No one. She runs back toward the boathouse. Frantic.

O.S., ducks suddenly FLAP up before her. Her car key goes flying. She lets out another blood curdling SCREAM, flailing, barely staying on her feet.

From the look on her face, her life as she knows it is about to come to an abrupt end.

**Lights to Black**

**Lights Up on Gazebo - Continuing**

She makes it back to her table in the gazebo and packs up her computer. Puts the letter opener in her bag.

BO comes out to the gazebo to find MARLEY searching her purse for something. He rushes to her.

MARLEY
Goddamn key, where are you?

BO
Marley? Honey?

MARLEY
Don't come over here.

BO
What's going on?

MARLEY
Just stay away. Go back into the house until I'm gone.

BO
Gone? Marley, this is crazy. Where are --

MARLEY
-- Bo, if you come any closer, I swear....

BO moves towards her. MARLEY goes for her bag.

BO grabs her. She pulls the letter opener out of it. And pushes him over the gazebo table.

They CRASH to the deck together. MARLEY on top of him, holding the opener to his throat.

BO
If this is some kind of crazy foreplay, it's not working.

MARLEY
There's a man dead in the lake. Hooman. He's been strangled. He left me a note to meet him. Now he's dead. I'm getting out of here. Before I'm next.

BO
Marley --

MARLEY
-- Shut up. Just roll over.

BO
Shit, come on --

MARLEY
-- Roll over!

BO rolls over and MARLEY uses the phone charger cord to tie his hands.

BO
This doesn't make a lick of sense.

MARLEY
It makes perfect sense from my end.

BO
Apparently. Just tell me why we can't talk this out.

MARLEY
Don't play stupid with me, Bo. Where's the other key?

BO

Marley --

MARLEY

(puts the letter opener back to his throat)

-- My goddamn car key.

BO

In my pocket. Marley.... What did Hooman tell you?

MARLEY

(finds the key)

Why don't we ask your mother, Bo? Oh, that's right, she's missing, murdered by your best friend. Wasn't she?

BO

I... it wasn't Sal's.... She... please, it was an accident. I should've told you. The guy... Marley. I don't know exactly, he... she was leaving Pop. Making him sell the business. Taking her half of everything and leaving. She had a gun, and Sal protected himself. We did what we had to. To keep things the way they were. Pop never knew. He thinks she just left.

The rain hits. They talk over it. They keep dry in the gazebo.

MARLEY

Just shut up, Bo. I don't know what you and Salvador are up to. But I'm not waiting around to find out why you two covered up your mother's death.

BO

Who would want to harm you? What's happening here?

(rolls on his side to face her)

Just tell me this. Who the hell are you?

MARLEY

(almost blurts it out, but she stops)

You son-of-a-bitch. I love you.

MARLEY stands up to leave. She wants to stay. But knows she can't. She runs to the house.

BO

Marley. Goddamnit. Let me explain. Let me help. Don't end it this way. Don't run.

MARLEY comes bursting back out the front door. Unfortunately, the SHERIFF is waiting for her.

SHERIFF

Marley?!

MARLEY walks towards the O.S. parking. The SHERIFF goes after her. Catching up at a near run.

SHERIFF

Marley. Wait. Jesus Christ... let's get out of the rain.

MARLEY

What is it, Sheriff?

(tries to step around him)

SHERIFF

Come on, now. Give me a minute.

MARLEY

I'm in a hurry.

SHERIFF

I can see that. You want to explain why your newspaper articles are scattered at the end of the dock, where we found a body of one of your workers floating in the lake?

MARLEY stops. What can she do?

SHERIFF

That is Hooman, are you aware of that?

MARLEY

Yes.

SHERIFF

(waits for more)

Don't make me have to read you your rights.

Just then, BO comes storming up. He stops when he sees the SHERIFF and MARLEY

**End of ACT II**
**Scene Two**

**ACT II**
**Scene Three**

**Lights up on McClure House**

Int. Ext. McClure House/Gazebo - Later. The rain has passed. SAM sits across the table BO gave MARLEY from the SHERIFF.

SHERIFF
Relax, Sam, just tell me slowly.

SAM
All I know is that Hooman was a hard working young man. He's worked for me and my father since he was a kid. He walked off suddenly and didn't come back. So I walked to the lake to where he often feeds the ducks with bread from his lunch. I heard a scream and saw Marley running away in a frenzied state before I got there.

SHERIFF
Alone?

SAM
At first, I thought Hooman had an accident. Then I thought, why were they together. Then didn't know what to think. Then that. The cord around his neck. Dead. Why?

SHERIFF
(moves to the door)
You mind sticking around until I have someone take your statement?

SAM
Marley and Bo, they couldn't've done this. Bo was up at the house. Hell, Marley, she's a lady. Hooman may've been dim, but he'da put up a hell'va fight. You should talk with this man Salvador Turk. Bo's friend. Heard them arguing.

SHERIFF
Just sit tight. I'll talk to everyone.

The SHERIFF goes outside to the gazebo and sits in front of MARLEY. He's not satisfied.

SHERIFF
Alright, Marley. Why all of a sudden leave town? Why not stay here and get help?

MARLEY
I panicked.

SHERIFF
That's putting it mildly.

MARLEY
Sheriff, you go to a remote place to meet a man who wants to tell you something important under thunder and lightening. And you find him dead. What would you do?

SHERIFF
I certainly wouldn't flee town leaving my new husband behind.

MARLEY
Sure, you're a man with a gun. I didn't know what to think. Surely, you don't think I killed him.

SHERIFF
Of course not, Marley... I just... why don't you go on back to the paper. Probably missed your deadline as it is. If I have questions, I'll get back to you on it. Gonna give Jaclyn a heart attack you keep working up here.

MARLEY gets up to leave.

SHERIFF
You have no idea why Hooman wanted to talk?

MARLEY
I thought it had something to do with the house. I'm paying out a lot of money, Sheriff. If I'm being ripped off. I want to know by whom.

SHERIFF
Are we talking Sam, Bo, or this Salvador Turk character?

MARLEY
Does it matter? Look, I have to work things out with Bo. Can we talk later? Give me an hour.

SHERIFF
Alright. I'll be back in an hour.

The SHERIFF is even less satisfied.

But MARLEY heads for the house, past a window.

BO is working on a piece of furniture. He's using a LOUD band saw. He watches her go by.

She gives him a hard look. MARLEY enters from the back. He doesn't see her. The saw WHINES to a stop.

MARLEY
Who knows I'm here?

BO
Shit, Marley. Make me cut off a thumb, why don't you.

MARLEY
Who knows, Bo?

BO
Just me and Salvador, at this point.

MARLEY
But you asked questions. Had people looking.

BO
No. Just Salvador.

MARLEY
Why?

BO
I have the right to know who I'm married to.

MARLEY
You bastard. You don't trust me?

She runs to the gazebo, packing her things. BO has no choice other than to stop her by climbing out a window.

MARLEY pulls away, runs back into the house. BO'S right behind her.

Running through the house.

MARLEY wanting to barricade herself in room-after-room. But to her announce, there's no locks on the doors.

BO opens doors after door until she has no escape. Finally the master bedroom door locks. She runs to the window where they made love.

BO
(at the locked door)
It's not what you think. With-all my heart, I love you.

MARLEY
Then who killed Hooman? Sal?

BO
Long as it wasn't you or me, we're okay.

MARLEY
How much do you know?

BO
You're in some kind of a Witness Protection Program.

MARLEY
Do you know why?

BO
No.

MARLEY
You liar.

BO
Okay, I know it had to do with the death of your parents. I know there's a price on your head. And involved your writing.

MARLEY
And your friend knows.

BO
Salvador's a little slow at times, but he's very good at finding out things. He came to me with an article that had a photo that looked like a younger you. I asked him to look into it. I didn't really care at the time. I was just keeping him busy. He was protecting --

MARLEY
-- He watched us through the window that night?

BO
No. He was at his place. I gave --

MARLEY
-- You gave him my fingerprints?

BO
Marley.... On a fork.

MARLEY
My fork?. You gave him my fork?!

BO
Yeah, I didn't know --

MARLEY
-- You moron. That fork belonged to my Great Grandmother. The set is a family heirloom from Austria. I've been looking all over for it. I can't believe this. You --

BO
-- To hell with your damn fork. I made a mistake. I tried to take the package back from him --

MARLEY
-- You gave him my fork the night you made love to me?

BO
Now, Marley, I know how this sounds.

MARLEY
You obviously don't! You, dumb son-of-a-bitch.

BO
I told him to stop. That I didn't want to know. If you'd just been honest with me. I wouldn't've --

MARLEY
-- screw you. I was protecting you. I was protecting us. What we have together. This life. And you --

BO
-- This isn't getting us anywhere.

MARLEY
You were pissed. And you wanted the house. Admit it.

BO
Okay. Yes. I wanted the house. But I didn't agree to go along with this. It's not why I married you.

MARLEY kicks the door. Startling him.

BO
I do love you, Marley, just know that. I can't help you if you don't believe me. I don't know what else to do? Tell me what we should do.

But no answer from MARLEY.

BO
Okay. I'll go talk it over with the Sheriff. Confess to being an idiot. I haven't done anything illegal.
(heads down the staircase)

MARLEY
Other than hide the death of your mother.

BO
Fine, it's time I came clean. I made a mistake not turning Sal in. My mother deserves better. If I see time, I'll deserve it. If you've got to run, you better start now.

MARLEY
(quickly thinks, realizing)
Bo. Don't do this. Don't go. I'll trust you. I'll find a way. Bo... you can't tell them who I am. We won't be safe here.

But BO is out the door. MARLEY follows, down the stares, and outside.

At the gazebo... she catches up with Bo.

MARLEY
Bo... I'm sorry, I should've told you. I just didn't know how. I was afraid they'll find me and hurt you.

They hug as though afraid to let go.

BO
Then we're in this together? The big whatevers. All the way to the end. Okay?

MARLEY
Yes. But we can't go to the Sheriff about Salvador. Once my cover is blown, I'm gone. I don't even know if they'll let me take you with me. There's a lot more to this.

BO
Then we've got to talk to Salvador.

MARLEY
Can we prove he killed Hooman?

BO
I'd say it's a fair chance. We need to convince him to keep silent. To stay away from us. Or we tell.

MARLEY
He'll still want his house. He knows all about us.

BO doesn't answer.

MARLEY
Are you sure that's all Salvador wants?

BO
Let's hope so. The article he showed me. Marley, these people you wrote about, what were you thinking they would do?

MARLEY
Nothing. I was simply basing a character on Semyon Lebedev a Russian Oligarch my father spoke of at dinner once. This fictional character I created, or so I thought, was trying to sell stolen data from Russian nuclear tests to Iraq.

BO
That’s not a new threat on the world. Why kill your parents?

MARLEY
I thought I was just being a thorough journalist writing her first possible fictional spy novel when I stumbled onto declassified information on how Israel’s covert operations acquired materials that lead to their producing weapons-grade plutonium many years ago. So, I copied the how it was done for my story, changing countries and names, to make it sound authentic.

BO
So, who’s after you... Russians or Israelis?

MARLEY
That’s just it. I was young and naive wanting be a best seller. Until I handed in my first draft to my publisher and they gave my research to the CIA. And suddenly, Semyon Lebedev was put in a Russian prison for life where someone eventually knifed him.

BO
And your parents were involved, how?

MARLEY
The information I found was in my father’s home office. On his desk. We never spoke about it, but I’m sure he unofficially left it there to help me with my book. Because he participated in organizations that supported the U.S.-Israel relationship, participating in think tanks and advocacy groups, he had access to this kind if information. Lebedev may have killed my parents from jail. For revenge. Because the tickets were in my name, someone might have thought I was on that plane. But it could’ve been ordered from Iraq or Israel... leaked by the person he got the information from. The CIA claims they don’t know. Or are not willing to tell me. But my father was somehow involved and someone murdered my parents from halfway around the world because of it. And I got my life taken away.

BO
So now, thanks to stupid woodchuck me, it could happen again.

MARLEY
We need to know what Salvador wants. Or we should run now. You will not be able to protect me from whoever is looking.

BO
Come on. Let's get out of the yard.

Bo leads her towards McClure House.

MARLEY
Are you sure Salvador hasn't let anyone else know who I am?

BO thinks it over.

MARLEY
Has he, Bo?

BO
I guess there's only one way to find out for sure.

**Lights to Black**

**Lights Up - Master Bedroom**

Int. McClure House - Night. In the master bedroom, BO reads a text on his phone. Marley is with him.

BO
He's coming here. Now.

But SALVADOR already stands outside the master bedroom door. Listening.

MARLEY
He's trying to put himself between us.

BO
My shop, your paper, this house, I agree. We can't let him take all this away from us.

MARLEY
Are you listening to me? We'll have to shut him up.

BO
I've known him my whole life, Marley....

MARLEY
(lowers her voice)
I'm talking money... we can't kill him... can we?

BO
If it was only that simple.

BO turns to find MARLEY looking at the door. Someone's there.

SALVADOR knocks. BO goes to the door.

BO
Look, Salvador, this is a mistake.

SALVADOR
Don't make me yell out here. People can here.

MARLEY
Don't let him in.

SALVADOR kicks the door open. He's got a gun.

BO
Damn it, Sal. I Just made that door.

SALVADOR
Quietly. Move back.

At gunpoint they back to the window where they first made love.

SALVADOR
You see, Bo. She's no good for us. She's trying to get you to kill me. She'll get everything then. All our work. She'll twist us two, our friendship, what we did, how you helped me, and still get all this, all my precious wood, all your beautiful work, because you're married. She used us. She'll make people think sick things. When it ain't that way.

BO
Sal --

SALVADOR
-- This was our house. She's just like your mom. Taking everything away again. Changing things. Throwing us out. Because she doesn’t really love us.

MARLEY starts to speak. BO stops her with a hand.

BO
Sal, it's not... she's not leaving.

MARLEY
Sal killed your mother so she wouldn't take your father's paint stores in the divorce? He murdered her, Bo. We can prove that if he doesn't leave us alone. Tell him!

BO
This isn't helping, Marley. It was an accident.

MARLEY
So you accidentally let him bury her?

(BO doesn't answer.)

SALVADOR
You told her? You know I was just trying to make her stay. Take this gun from her.

BO
You told me you got rid of her gun.

SALVADOR
I didn't.

SALVADOR raises the gun. Points it at MARLEY.

BO
I know, I know... wait, it's okay, wait, wait. Salvador, wait. She found out on her own. I didn't tell her. Give me a second to think --

SALVADOR
-- You got two. One --

BO
-- No matter what happens, it will be me they come looking for. We won't have this together. We'll have no place to hide. They'll put me away, too.

SALVADOR
You wanted wood. I got you wood. You promised me I'd always have a home here if I got you the wood you needed to rebuild your dream home. Well, I have dreams, too. And I had to do things you don't want to know about to make yours come true. That's why I kept your name out of it. Now she has everything. And you're telling me I've got no place to go? That my dreams are no good anymore?

BO
I didn't see this coming, Sal.

SALVADOR
She doesn't want me. She won't let me put my house out back. She wants it all for herself. Givin' my lot to the city. Leavin' those bodies on it. She's not good for us. She's not right about us. This ain't right about anything we planned.

BO
Okay, Salvador. I'm in. Just --

MARLEY
-- What?!

BO
Give me a second, Marley.

SALVADOR
You in, you kill her.

BO
Okay. There's no other way out. I can see that.

MARLEY
Bo?

SALVADOR
Good. So, how do we do it?

MARLEY
Bo?!

BO
I'm sorry, Marley. I don't want to die over this just because you have to. Your friends will find you eventually.

SALVADOR
This is the 'till death do we part-part.

MARLEY
But you said --

BO
-- I do love you. What choice do I have? There's all this work still to be done on this place. One of us has to see it through. It's got to be me.

MARLEY
You son-of-a-bitch. You liar!

BO
Give me Mother's gun, Salvador.

SALVADOR
What? No.

BO
Sal, it's me, Bo. You know I'd never hurt you. Now give me the gun. Let me finish it. I helped you before when we were punk teenagers. Didn't I? Lied for you. Told you how to dig a deep hole under the tree roots. I did that to protect you. Protect us and Pop. To keep things the way they were. Right?

SALVADOR
(stops to think it out)
Snap her neck with your hands, then. Like I accidently did Mother when Pop told me to bring her back. Then I'll know for sure. I'll leave town and go work with Pop for a spell. Take her body with me and bury it back home. Deep in the woods like before. Once the tree roots get to her, she'll stay gone forever. Even them Russians won't find her.

BO
Then you shoot her. You want me to do it. Give me the gun. I can't have her looking at me while I choke her. I can't listen to her neck snap like that, I can't. Otherwise, you do it.

SALVADOR
No. You must kill her. Do her any way you can. I don't care. She dies, the house is ours. We'll find a way to fix all this. We'll tell 'em the Russians got her. But I'm not givin' you this gun. Just show me you're in this all the way. So we can make it like it was. Just you and me again.

BO
Then we got a situation here.

MARLEY
Bo? Think this through. You won't get the house. First your mother. Now your wife. It'll all piece together. They'll check my computer, see what I've been reading about you.

BO
This isn't personal. It's business. Sal didn't mean to kill my mother. Did you, Sal? Sal?

But Sal doesn't answer.

MARLEY
It's lunacy. You'll both end up with life behind bars.

SALVADOR
Use that board. Beat her with it.

BO
Salvador, come on. Are you listening to yourself? That's soft pine. I'll have to hit her several times. She'll scream. You've heard her scream. Blood all over the damn place. We won't be able to hide that.

SALVADOR
Cops will think the people looking for her did it. Hell, if I found her. Anyone can find her.

BO
You did good, Sal. You did real good. But we --

SALVADOR
-- Once I started poking around on the internet. I was in. Look at her. They're looking for Tammy Wright. Well, here she is. Fingerprints don't lie. We found her. Anyone could find here. Says she was writing some investigative spy novel on nuclear weapons. We don't really know her. Could be a spy. You see it? It could work. Just you and me, Bo. Like it was. As surprised as anyone about who she is and what she's hiding.

BO

Okay, Sal. I see it. You done good. We'll put your place further out back. Forget the third house. We got the park. We got her money. I'm her husband. I'll get everything.

SAL

Right, we don't need a third house. We got her money. But it ain't like we planned. We'll just put my house out back.

BO

Just give me the gun. Let me get this over with. Come on, be flexible.

SALVADOR'S still not sure. Wants to. But it just doesn't seem right in his head yet.

**Lights Up on Ext. McClour House**

Ext. the house, SAM stops down below looking up at the window. He's looking at the unhappy shadows from the work light in the window.

BO bends down and picks up the two-by-four. Feels it. Soft grain. It'll have to do.

MARLEY starts backing away. She glances out the window to see SAM move to the house.

BO

It's okay, Marley. I've got to do this. I'll be quick. Just trust I really love you.

MARLEY

Sure you don't want to strangle me like Salvador did Hooman?

SALVADOR

I done it for us, Bo.

BO

You had to, Sal. I know.

SALVADOR is forced to move closer to MARLEY to keep her still. Slowly they corner her. BO draws back with the board. MARLEY cringes.

The Child's GHOSTLY GIGGLE from behind them. SALVADOR turns to look. SAM is at the door.

SAM

What the hell's...?

BO whacks SAL in the head, again... and again.

BO grabs up MARLEY and pushes SAM toward the door. They run for it as SALVADOR stumbles back against the bay window, barely keeping from falling.

**Lights to Black on Master Bedroom**

**Lights Up on Backyard Gazebo/Dock/Boathouse/Lake**

They run fast. But SAM isn't the fleetest of guys and falls down. BO comes back for him.

SALVADOR is already out of the house. He's hurt bad.

He's got blood running down his face. Takes that moment to cut them off. Forcing them to go along the dock to the bottomless lake.

SALVADOR is right behind them, falling, getting up, stopping to steady himself. He's a mess.

They reach the brick boathouse and the docks. Bo looks around for a weapon and finds a broken brick used to hold the boathouse door.

MARLEY

This is crazy. What are we doing here?

BO

We've got to end this. Can you swim?

MARLEY

Not in a dark bottomless lake at night.

BO

He won't follow. Water frightens him.

SAM

We'll be sitting ducks out there.

BO

We already are. Unless you get in the water. Right now, dive. I'll wait for him. Go.

Shows them the brick. BO kicks off his shoes. Takes off his shirt.

**Lights to Black on BO, SAM and MARLEY**

**Lights Up on SALVADOR and BO**

SALVADOR reaches the docks, stumbles. Falling. Fighting to keep his feet. Crying.

SALVADOR

You lied to me, Bo. I trusted you. Bo? I need you. I'm bleeding. I'm hurt. Help me. Bo, please. Get me home to Pop. She's no good for us. She's... just like Mother. Bo, please don't do this... help me... we're family, I'll kill her for you, Bo. I can still kill her. It's not too late. It can still be like we....

O.S. SPLASHING comes from out in the lake.

SALVADOR

Bo?

Behind him Bo steps into the faint light. He's got the brick. He makes a move to...

... but SALVADOR sees BO's shoes and shirt, stumbles further out on the dock. Blood in his SALVADOR'S eye.

O.S., MARLEY and SAM are swimming away.

SALVADOR

Bo!

(sees only two swimmers)

What did they...? BO..!

He goes to the end of the dock. It's clear he doesn't like the water... especially in the dark. He aims the gun at MARLEY and SAM. Starts shooting.

O.S., SAM cries out. MARLEY swims harder.

SALVADOR moves back toward the brick boathouse, searching the water for BO when, WHAM. He gets slammed with the loose brick from behind, dropping the gun, as he fights to stand.

BO picks up his shirt, using it to pick up the gun. No prints. Points it at Sal.

Sal crumbles to his knees. Confused. Reaching up.

SALVADOR

But... I always loved you, Bo.

BO

I know, Sal. I love you, too.

They smile at each other. This is goodbye.

Lights to Black on Bo and Salvador

Gun shot!

**End of ACT II**
**Scene Three**

**ACT II**
**Scene Four**

**Lights Up on McClure House**

Ext. McClure House/Gazebo - Beautiful Day. Early Spring. Birds Chirping. The house is done. Magnificent grand old place.

Bo and Marley are at the Gazebo - Life is good.

Until O.S., SHERIFF'S car pulls up. A door SLAMS. SHERIFF enters stage. He's not happy. He stops and looks at the house. Then to his once happy town. He heads for the gazebo.

MARLEY and BO are there drinking ice tea. They both look up and see the look on the SHERIFF'S face.

SHERIFF
They found Sam.

MARLEY
Sam? Is he...?

SHERIFF
Out in the lake. Far side, on county land. All fenced off. Hard to get to, all the brush and what not. Ducks and rodents have eaten most of him after the ice melted. But it's him.

BO
How?

SHERIFF
Hard to say the way he looks. They'll dredge for his truck.

BO
Have you called his family?

SHERIFF
They're on their way. They found another. Buried along the lake shore. Shot in the head. Apparent suicide. Wrapped in heavy plastic, though.

MARLEY
That's terrible.

SHERIFF
Yeah, isn’t it. Wisconsin gas receipts in his pocket. Might be your friend. You two wouldn't know anything about this, would you?

MARLEY
Why would we?

SHERIFF
Bo's Wisconsin friend. Sam was your architect. Little things like that.

MARLEY
I just hired Sam. I don't know what else he was into. Perhaps he --

SHERIFF
-- I've known Sam a long time. Knew his daddy before him. Watched all his kids grow to be fine people. Sam wasn't into anything other than saving these old homes.

BO
He was a good man. Salvador was --

SHERIFF
-- an odd fellow, for sure. As you know, we've been lookin' for him since Hooman was murdered.

BO
All we know is he and I argued over being outbid on the wood we needed, and he took off. I don't speak to my pop, so I don't know if he went back home or not. We haven't heard from him since. You don't think -

SHERIFF
-- Tryin' not to think anything until I get all the facts.

MARLEY
As you know, Bo and I had to finish the house on our own. We couldn't bear to hire anyone else after Sam went missing.

SHERIFF
Done a fine job, too. The forensic investigation will hopefully bring everything to light. In the meantime, I hope you two aren't plannin' a vacation. In case we need your help to sort this all out.

BO
We're here to stay, Sheriff.

SHERIFF
Yep, the rest of your lives, I hope.

MARLEY
It's hot. Can we get you anything? Ice tea?

SHERIFF
I'm good. I'll let you know what we find. Could take a day or two.

Sheriff Brown turns and leaves.

BO
(makes sure they're alone)
What do you think?

MARLEY
Your call. I'm with you. Run or stay. If they won't let us stay together, we're on our own.

BO
It's gonna be like this, isn't it.

MARLEY
It'll come and go.

BO
It's a perfect haunted house.

MARLEY
I couldn't invent a better life. Last chance. Killing Salvador was self-defense. He had a gun, killed Sam.

BO
Yeah, but burying him in that tarp already has them looking at us.

MARLEY
He killed your mom. He admitted it. You don't have to give all this away because of me.

BO
I'm not. Being the right man to save McClour House made me find you. I couldn't live here alone, knowing I let you go. My guess, they're building a case against both of us right now.

MARLEY
Then don't worry, Sam's family will take good care of Arrow. And keep your shop open.

BO
I know, the kids love him. But still....
(sees Marley tearing, wipes it)
Hey, it's okay, you can write your book anywhere. And Jaclyn and Judy will keep your paper alive, too. Maybe even Matthew employed without hurting him too much.

They smile, slightly, knowing this is the end of McClour House for them.

MARLEY
Then we made the right choice. Sam would've been proud of us.

BO
It was his dream to leave McClour House to his family.

MARLEY
As long as we have each other.

MARLEY takes BO's hand, kisses her.

BO
Somewhere there's a home for us.

A FLASH in the upstairs window. They look. A figure of the young boy stands in the window. He smiles sadly, waves, and fades. Off their surprised reaction.

**Lights Fade to Black**

**CURTAIN**

# Bonjour, America

A Neo-Noir Sensory-Immersive Thriller Stage Play

(based on the screenplay)

by

Karl J. Niemiec

## CHARACTERS

**VINCENT BOYET:** Twenty-five. Clean cut, French suit salesman, wears dark rimmed glasses. He has a deathly fear of heights and water. In a panic, after a tire blowout, he drove his rented car and family's French suit sample collection off a bridge into a river. He's hitch hiking, trying to get home to Salt Lake City to his pregnant wife.

**DANE MORGAN:** Forties. Local dishonest Sheriff, laundering Cincinnati Mob money through the local bank. He's also a hard living, forth generation good old boy pig farmer.

**QUINNLY SULLIVAN:** Twenty-six. A dirty hot-sex about her that collects losers like dust to a TV. Waitress at the Spoon Café. Her and her boyfriend got off the train and he supposedly took off and left her there.

**TRAVIS HIGHTOWER:** 30s, scruffy - Grifter bank robber.

**LEONARDO HIGHTOWER:** 30's. Travis' cousin. Grifter bank robber, pool player.

**JEREMIAD JOHNSTONE:** 30s. Small town lawyer, pool player.

**ELI TWAIN:** Fifties. A bullish very peculiar, hairy neck, smelly chicken rancher.

**BLAIR MOULDS:** 30s. Balding redneck. A short-order cook and owner of the Spoon Café.

**CHERYL MOULDS:** 20s. Blair's wife and waitress at the Spoon Café.

**ZACHARY:** 70s. He's owner of General Dry Goods Store.

**TRULY DUNN:** 30s. She works the counter at Driftwood Whistle Inn. A plump, pleasant woman, with exquisite breast. Otherwise bland as applesauce.

**STATIONMASTER:** 90s. A hunched-over, ghostly willow of a man. He wears a vintage dark train conductor's suit and cap.

**BROOKE:** 20s. A rail of a woman. Works at the Poolhall/Bar.

**DEPUTY SHERIFF TOMCAT REILLY:** 30s. A cruel drunk bastard. One hundred pounds over weight. Cheating on his wife with Brooke.

**BARTENDER:** 50s. Missing an arm and an eye.

**SHERI BOYET:** 20s. V.O. performed by one of the other female characters.

**SETTING:**

If time stood still, it would expire here and turn into pig farming, chicken rancher dust. These people are lost in unfriendly shadows of a nothing-town's underworld-money laundering scheme that's gone on far too long. Located in colorless America that's stuck to bleached-out Driftwood Crossing, Colorado - Founded 1872 - Population: 34 1/2.

The sets can be bare boned, exposed by dimly lit moments as lights go up and down to quicken the pace and bridge between continuing scenes from multiple concurrent scenes and sets.

**Sets:** a near ghost town, rundown and decaying, Spoon Café, Driftwood Crossing Flophouse, its Lobby/Poolhall/Bar/Alley, all in and around that one building, with an Int. Bank across the street. Other sets exposed by dim light: Crossroads, Boxcar, Ext. Vincent's Salt Lake City Home.

**TIME:**

The hot, dry Summer of 1960.

**ACTS - SCENES:**

The use of minimal sets and props is discretionary and up to the production.

**ACT I - Scene One -** American Crossroads/Spoon Café - Sunset

**ACT I - Scene Two -** Driftwood Whistle - Evening

**ACT I - Scene Three -** Driftwood Whistle - Night

**ACT I - Scene Four -** Three Driftwood Whistle Rooms - Night

**ACT I - Scene Five -** Driftwood Lobby/Poolhall/Bar/Alley/ Crossroads - Night

**ACT II - Scene One -** Spoon Café - Daybreak

**ACT II - Scene Two -** Ext. Driftwood Crossing/Int. Bank - Day

**ACT II - Scene Three -** Ext.Int. Boxcar/Plowed Field - Day

**ACT II - Scene Four -** Int. Driftwood Whistle Lobby - Night

**ACT II - Scene Five -** Ext. Vincent's Home - Night

**At Rise:**

**ACT I**
**Scene One**

**Ext. American Crossroad - Sunset**

Middle of the Summer 1960.

O.S., heading West, a rust-eaten 1940's Chevy chugs and squeaks to a sudden brake-grinding stop.

VINCENT BOYET, 25, steps into the light. His fine European suit badly torn. Spotted with river muck. Knees ragged. Elbows bloodied.

The Chevy drives on O.S. Destined for a ring job. Dust and fumes hit Vincent hard on a hot gust. He cleans his dark rimmed glasses, squints, taking in his new predicament.

He's at the south end of a sunbaked gravel road sloping north a quarter mile through a no-light, bleached-wood town in the middle of dried up, nowhere America.

Vincent looks down at his feet. He's got one dress shoe.

Then looks back at the no-where town. With a Parisian French accent...

VINCENT

Bonjour, America.

With misgiving, he takes a step and stops in front of a badly Sun blanched sign: "DRIFTWOOD CROSSING, COLORADO" FOUNDED 1872.

Vincent brushes away dust. Revealing: chalky rock marks counting down the town's population: 37, 36, 35, 341/2.

Under it is scratched: Don't bother!

**Black on Cross Roads**

**Lights Up on Driftwood Crossing**

Ext./Int. "SPOON CAFÉ". But the half lit buzzing neon sign over a screen door reads "SPOO C E - Daybreak. Vincent stops under it.

He turns away from stacks of O.S. stinking cages filled with RESTLESS CHICKENS on a vintage flatbed.

Sheriff, DANE MORGAN, 40's, exits the Café. He's from generations of hard living good-old-boy pig farmers.

JEREMIAD JOHNSTONE, 30's, a small time mouthy lawyer, follows. The chicken smell hits them hard.

DANE

Jesus Christ, Eli.

ELI (O.S.)

As I told you, Sheriff. I keeps 'em where I can sees 'em.

Dane lets the door SLAP behind him.

DANE

Dim-witted son-of-a --

JEREMIAD (O.S.)

-- Ought to throw a barbecue.

ELI (O.S.)

Be the last chicken you ever choked.

Vincent and Dane eye each other as they pass. Their stark contrast as lucent and broken as the BUZZING neon.

Jeremiad exits the Café, making Vincent step out of his way. Shoving in a wad of chew, he walks over to the next door in the same building leading into The Driftwood Whistle Inn/Poolhall/Bar.

He turns at the SLAP of the Café screen door as Vincent goes inside to find that Dane isn't following.

JEREMIAD

Damn.... Come on, Dane.

DANE
I gotta run up to the house and make a few calls.

JEREMIAD
Shit, I'll spot you three stripies.

DANE
Find someone else to persecute tonight, J.J., I don't need you squeezing my balls.

Jeremiad laughs as Dane watches Vincent inside the Spoon Café. He's not happy to see him.

Meanwhile, Int. Spoon Café, Vincent has made his way into the front empty booth. The lack of a shoe makes it awkward.

Two scruffy first cousins, TRAVIS and LEONARDO HIGHTOWER, 30's, finish up their meals at the counter. "Grifting losers" written all over them.

ELI TWAIN, 50's, sits in a booth by the window. A bullish peculiar, hairy neck guy. An oddly fitted plaid wool cap with chicken feathers on his head. He uses his fat tongue to noisily get the last ice cube out of his glass.

ELI
Can I have more water? You got more water, Quinnly? I could use water.

QUINNLY SULLIVAN, 26, in a tight fitting diner uniform, stacks glasses behind the counter. A dirty hot-sex about her that collects losers like dust to a TV.

QUINNLY
Shut up, Eli. You can see I'm occupied.

She gives Vincent the "one too many losers in this place already" look, as she swats the two grifters with her towel.

LEONARDO
The hell was that for?

QUINNLY
(grabs up a menu)
Travis, tell your dumb-ass cousin the next time he touches himself whilst givin' me the dirty eye, I'll take it out.

LEONARDO
I got me a heat rash.

QUINNLY
(plops a menu down for Vincent)
I'll give you a heat rash.
(picks up a tip from Dane)

TRAVIS
Where ya suppose he got it from?

Quinnly refills Eli's water. She shoots Travis a warning. He turns back around. He says something inaudible to Leonardo.

LEONARDO
Shuddup.

QUINNLY
You've peed three times since you been here, Eli.

ELI
Eight glasses a day. That's what the doc says. I got an enlarged prostate.

QUINNLY
He say anything about water on the brain?

ELI
(looks at his glass)
Nah, can't happen to a man. Can it?

QUINNLY
(goes back behind the counter)
None I met in this town.

TRAVIS
Come on, Leonardo, we don't have to take this kind of misuse.

LEONARDO
Damn straight. If I needed snapped by a floozy I'd'a stayed livin' with your mamma.

Vincent reads the menu.

The two grifters laugh their way to the door. Leonardo walks with a clubfoot.

Travis turns to study Vincent, glancing at Quinnly. She motions them out, so they exit.

Vincent looks up to find Eli watching him. Vincent holds up his menu to hide behind it. After a moment Quinnly comes back.

QUINNLY
Never mind him. You ready to order, slick?

VINCENT
Oui, madame. The meatloaf special. Extra side of brown jus... gravy.

QUINNLY
Blair, we still got the special?

BLAIR MOULDS, 30's, lifts his balding redneck head into the order window.

BLAIR
I already told you, Quinnly.

QUINNLY
Boss says he's having the last.

VINCENT
Perhaps the trout. Poached if --

QUINNLY
-- Yeah, if we had it, but we don't. River's dry till October. Don't ask.

VINCENT
Okay, what does the boss suggest?

QUINNLY
He suggests ham and eggs. We got lots and lots of ham and eggs.

VINCENT
Super, I'll have three eggs up with home fries. Rye with jelly. Coffee black. Skip the ham.

QUINNLY
(writes it down)
That blood?

VINCENT
A little automobile trouble.

QUINNLY
Automobile. We don't get much foreign traffic.

VINCENT
You should post a sign.

QUINNLY
People would stop.

VINCENT
That's the idea. No?

QUINNLY
Not around these parts.

Eli stops at Vincent's table, doesn't say anything. Tips his cap. Exits. After a moment Eli's smell hits Vincent. Quinnly clears Eli's table. Pocket's the nickel tip.

VINCENT
Merci. Perhaps there's a local lodge where I could soak in a bathtub?

CHERYL, 20's, Blair's wife, enters from the back. Opens the register, counts money. Exchanges looks with Quinnly after eyeing Vincent.

QUINNLY
A flophouse and poolhall next door. The view's no more unpleasant than the clientele.

**Black on Café**

**End of ACT I**
**Scene One**

**ACT I**
**Scene Two**

**Lights Up on Driftwood Whistle Inn**

Int. The Driftwood Whistle Inn - Evening. Three-story wood framed flophouse. The Inn, Café, Bar, and Poolhall are within the same building. The place is twenty years past needing tearing down. It leans toward a O.S. rail track.

Vincent stands at the front check in counter.

Behind the counter is TRULY DUNN, 30's, plump with exquisite breast, otherwise bland as applesauce.

Through a bar door is a pool table and a bar. Jeremiad Johnson is drinking and playing pool alone. He looks up from the ball when he hears Truly speak.

TRULY
The only room we got available corners off at the tracks. I got to caution you. No one around here likes staying there.

VINCENT
No worries as long as there's a telephone, bathtub, and hot water.

TRULY
No guarantee on the hot water. Let it run awhile though, so's it clears up. You need to make a phone call, you pick up the phone, it rings here. I'm Truly. I dial the number for you, and live right back there. Don't drive me crazy. I'm off at nine. You can find me in the poolhall back there after that. But don't. Unless the place is on fire or you're buying.

VINCENT
That's fine, Truly.

TRULY
Sign here. Address and phone. That's eight-ten a night upfront. Calls are extra.

Vincent signs the registry book.

TRULY
Vincent Boyer. That French?

VINCENT
Oui, madame.

TRULY
Ain't you the soup de jour? Thought so.

VINCENT
You know French?

TRULY
Hell no. But I'm willing you buy me that drink.

VINCENT
Another time, perhaps.

TRULY
You dumb enough to come back this way, I'll buy you that drink. Open door at the second landing. Room thirteen.

VINCENT
(pays with cash)
A key?

TRULY
No key. Locks ain't worked in years.

VINCENT
Merci.

TRULY
You'll be fine. Ain't lost a Frenchman in months.

Of Vincent's reaction....

**Black on Lobby**

**Lights Up on Vincent's Room**

Vincent's room - Evening. He's using the phone. Spread out on the bed. His one shoe off.

VINCENT
Me too... Good night, my love... Do not worry... caress the belly. Oui, the moment I step off the train. Sleep well, mon amour.

Hangs up. Looks at himself in a mirror. Shirt has blood stains. His forehead, a cut above an eye. Scraped achy knees. Takes out the cash in his pocket. Not enough.

There's a knock at his door, startling Vincent. Dane stands at the opening door, looking Vincent over.

VINCENT
Bonjour, Sheriff. Vincent Boyer.

DANE
Had a fun day, I see.

VINCENT
Oui, a disagreement with my rental over how to cross a very angry river.

DANE
That right. Looks to me you lost.

VINCENT
Sadly, this is true. The tire gave out, and the car longed for a swim in the river. While I don't even wade through a fountain unless I'm hand in hand with someone I adore.

An uncomfortable moment as Vincent's joke falls flat.

DANE
You need a doctor, you're out'a luck.

VINCENT
No, I'm --

DANE
-- General Store and Train Station across the street are closed about now. But I'll have old Zachary and the Stationmaster stop up and help you set back on your journey.

VINCENT
Wouldn't want to bother --

DANE
-- No bother to me. They'll be up with something about your size and direction.

VINCENT
Wouldn't happen to know --

DANE
-- Probably not.

VINCENT
All right then. Was a pleasure to have met, Sheriff.

DANE
Don't go stirring up trouble, Frenchy.

Dane turns and leaves when he hears someone struggling to climb the stairs.

After a moment Zachary appears in the hall, winded from the climb. Looks at Vincent, until Vincent steps aside to let him in to plop clothing and boots on the bed.

VINCENT
Very kind of you...

ZACHARY
Kind hell, I'm up here making a sale.

VINCENT
Oui, of course.

Vincent goes through the shirt selections Zachary brought with him. There's an enormous contrast from what he's wearing and what his choices are. Nothing but Levi. Zachary watches Vincent closely as he examines the brass buttons on a Levi jacket. The buttonholes are very stiff.

VINCENT
Quaint little town.

ZACHARY
Stale bread stick can be quaint, depending what you make of it.

VINCENT
How very true. Some of this fabric must be ten years old. No?

ZACHARY
(suspicious look)
Ain't a day over eight. Levi is Levi unless it ain't Levi at all.

VINCENT
Very good, Levi it is.
(selects a Levi shirt, pants, and jacket.)

ZACHARY
(adds it all up.)
Good choice. Fifty-five even all together with the socks and boots. Lookin' at ya, those should all fit.

(Zachary takes Vincent's money. Gives him back change. Picks up the remaining clothing. Moves over to the open door. Zachary looks him over again.)

VINCENT
Merci.

ZACHARY
Welcome. Ask for an ass kickin' around these parts, you get one. Country American style.

VINCENT
Not on my list of things to do while lost in America.

ZACHARY
Good thinkin'. Traffic starts up again on the road about the time the crow cackles. Won't be much on Saturday if any.

VINCENT
Bright and early then. Gardez la foi.

Vincent tries to close the door but an old hand, stops it. Vincent steps out into the hall. No one.

STATIONMASTER
No one out there, I saw.

Vincent turns to find the STATIONMASTER, 90's, hunched over, willow of a man, in his room. Dark blue suit and cap from the stagecoach days.

VINCENT
Oh, pardon.

STATIONMASTER
(checks his pocket watch)
Times tickin'. You expectin' anyone else?

VINCENT
What? No. I wasn't positive I saw anyone at all.

STATIONMASTER
Well, did you?

VINCENT
Sorry?

STATIONMASTER
You believe in spooks, boy? This place is full of 'em, you look close enough. Something I can help you with?

VINCENT
Oui, I'd like to inquire about a ticket out of town, Mister --

STATIONMASTER
-- Stationmaster's good enough. Where to, young fella?

VINCENT
Salt Lake.

STATIONMASTER
Well now, might find one that will take you southwest to Vegas... but definitely not northwest to Salt Lake.

Could take the train and get off at Clear Water. Catch a bus from there.

VINCENT
At this point, it's important I get home.

STATIONMASTER
I see, big hurry, are we.

VINCENT
When is the next train?

STATIONMASTER
Train? Next train is due by in about two hours. But that's all it is, due by. The next passenger train ain't due in for another... oh...about...
(checks his pocket watch again)
...thirty-two hours, thirteen minutes, and five seconds. I could put you down for a ticket.

VINCENT
Well, I've got time to think this out.

STATIONMASTER
Oh, you got time to think. Not much else to do. Just don't think big ideas around here.

Stationmaster follows Vincent to the door. He pulls out a candle and a box of matches from his pocket.

STATIONMASTER
If I was you, young fella, I'd take this candle, pour me a nice hot bath, and sit in it as long as I could. Clear the spooks out of your head. Candle light does that to you.

VINCENT
Great then, I guess I'll take --

Stationmaster shuts the door in Vincent's face.

VINCENT
Spooks. In such an affectionate town?

**Black on Vincent's Room**

**End of ACT I**
**Scene Two**

**ACT I**
**Scene Three**

**Lights Up on Vincent's Bathroom**

Vincent turns off the bath water. Sitting in it under dim light from the door. Naked except a ring on his finger. Every muscle in his body aches. BUG LIFE beyond the window grows out of the silence.

Finally, sitting back enjoying the candlelight when low RUMPUSES from the other flophouse TENANTS seeps through the night's ambiance.

At first, just a lot of UNINTELLIGIBLE MURMUR, CUPBOARDS BANGING, WATER RUNNING. The walls and floors being paper-thin. But slowly, parts of the DISCUSSIONS from the rooms begin to solidify.

REILLY (O.S.

... tired of all this shit on.... wonder you got bugs.

**Lights Stay On in Vincent's Room**

**Lights Up in Brooke Hope's Room**

Third Floor infested dustbowl, a room right above Vincent' room - Night. BROOKE HOPE, 20's, rail thin, and DEPUTY SHERIFF TOMCAT P. REILLY, 40's, one hundred pounds over weight confront each other with angry faces.

BROOKE

Then get out. Go on back to your fat butt wife. See if I care.

Vincent tries not to listen, sliding down in the tub.

REILLY

Christ, you got a mouth. Look, this plate is from three nights ago. And Christ-oh mighty, look at the leg hair... you eat out of this sink.

BROOKE

That ain't leg hair, you ass.

**Black on Brooke Hope's room**

**Lights Remain Up on Vincent's Room**

Glass SMASHES O.S., on the floor above. Long spooky echoing SCREAM from a child that fades back into the couple up above now unintelligible... when from behind his headboard comes....

QUINNLY (O.S.)
I'm tired, call me later. I want to lie down...

**Lights Up on Quinnly's room - Continuing**

Quinnly's Second Floor room is right next to Vincent's. The headboards are against the same wall - Night.

Quinnly spreads out across the bed. Still in her work clothes. Half filled bottle of rye sits on the nightstand.

QUINNLY
... for a spell. Look, I don't sit around all day eating sticky buns. Fine... call me when you do.
SLAMS down the phone. Lights a cig.

**Black on Quinnly's room**

Vincent thinks... then from the bathroom next door on the other side of his room.

TRAVIS (O.S.)
Throw me one of them towels, Leo.

**Lights Remain Up in Vincent's Room**

**LightS Up on Leonardo's and Travis' Room - Continuing**

The Grifters' Second Floor Room - Night. Leonardo throws a towel out of the bathroom then sets himself to crap O.S. Travis cleans his GUN on the bed just outside the door.

LEONARDO (O.S.)
What're we gonna bathe with, you keep usin' them as rags?

TRAVIS
You ain't got enough towels call that plump-apple at the front desk.

Vincent reacts to hearing them so clearly by grabbing a towel and gets out of the tub to dry off O.S.

LEONARDO (O.S.)
I just might. That girl gets nasty, I'm tellin' you.

TRAVIS
Please don't. I just ate.

The toilet FLUSHES. Leonardo comes out of the bathroom wanting to dry his hands.

LEONARDO
Has a bright personality, too. The way she mentioned being in the bar... so we'd show up.

TRAVIS
For a pet maybe. And I got the feelin' she tells that to everybody 'cause she's desperate.

LEONARDO
Go about chasin' faces you be missin' a whole flatbed of good lovin'.

TRAVIS
Shiiiit. Gonna give me gout. The good she'll do you.

They sit a moment. Travis has his gun apart. Leonardo picks up Travis’s knife off the bed.

LEONARDO
(picks his nails with it)
How much do you figure that bank holds right about now?

TRAVIS
You hear how dumb you sound?

LEONARDO
What? I'm just passin’ time.

TRAVIS
Well, I ain't passin’ time six-feet under ‘cause you got anxious.

Vincent doesn't want to hear this as he exits the bathroom fully dressed in his Levi and boots.

LEONARDO
I couldn't give less a crap. I was just speculatin'.

Vincent moves over, sees himself in the mirror, shakes his head in disbelief, but owns it, getting a smile at himself out of it.

TRAVIS
Just shuddup, and put down my knife before you lop a finger.

Vincent sits on his bed. Leans over, looks in the drawer. Nothing but an ancient Bible. He lies down.

LEONARDO
Damn, look what you're doin' to all them towels.

**Black on Vincent's and the Drifters Rooms**

**End of ACT I**
**Scene Three**

**ACT I**
**Scene Four**

**Lights up on Vincent's Room**

After a fitful sleep, MOANING wakes Vincent, coming through the wall from Quinnly's room. She's getting it good. Her headboard starts POUNDING on the wall.

Vincent puts his pillow over his head as Dane loudly orgasms like a pig in heat.

**Lights Up on Quinnly's Room**

Dane rolls off Quinnly. In a fit of sweat. Reaches for her cigs. He lights two. He puts one in Quinnly's mouth. She takes a drag. He takes it out and tries to kiss her. She blows smoke at him and pushes his face away. Taking the cig back.

QUINNLY
You know I hate that.
(pours the last of the rye)

DANE
What? It's a kiss.

QUINNLY
Your stash gives me hives. And your mouth stinks of pig shit and pussy.

DANE
Jesus... so I'll shave it.

QUINNLY
Just don't kiss me.

DANE
All right, all right, shit you're a screwed up broad. What's the matter? Your daddy used to give you hives?

QUINNLY
Piss-off. You want to kiss something, kiss my ass.

They sit in silence for a moment, smoking. Dane is shaking his head, not wanting to antagonize her. He finishes the last of his rye and eyes the empty bottle.

Vincent rolls over, enjoying the moment of silence, when....

DANE
This time tomorrow things are gonna change, goddamn it. Leave all them stinking pigs to my brother. I got it all worked out.

QUINNLY
If I had an orgasm for every dumb son-of-a-bitch who's told me that.

Dane pulls on his boxer shorts and moves over to the bathroom. Turns on the WATER in the tub and WASHES his penis at the sink.

DANE
Honey, there ain't no one in this county who hasn't profited from this arrangement, one way or another.

Dane exits the bathroom. His belly hanging out. Not an overly attractive man by any means.

QUINNLY
You got this all thunk out?

DANE
(putting on his pants)
You want money. I want you. Is that so bad?

QUINNLY
I'll let you know when I see my share.

Vincent removes the pillow, worried. Not sure what he just heard.

**Black on Quinnly's Room**

REILLY (UPSTAIRS O.S.)
Goddamn, woman. I didn't say put an ice cube in this. I said put some ice in it.

BROOKE (UPSTAIRS O.S.)
I ain't your waitress, you jackass. I gave you what ice there was. You see any in my drink?

A loud O.S. THUMP hits the floor above. Most likely her body. Followed by more broken glass.

REILLY (O.S.)
Get your skinny ass outfitted for work. Right now, or I'll give you more of this.

Vincent has heard enough. He gets out of bed and puts on the jean jacket as THUMPING and YELLING continue from up above.

BROOKE (O.S.)
I'll get dressed when I feel like it.

**Lights Up on Hallway**

Dane exits Quinnly's Room. Vincent opens his door. Finds himself face to face with Dane.

VINCENT
"Pardonne moi... the noise, I couldn't sleep.

DANE
Not to fret, I'm on my way to have a word with Reilly. About time for Brooke to go down to work anyway. You just enjoy the rest of your evening.

Vincent goes back into his room. Looks at the bed, then to the door. Worried.

A train whistle off in the distance. A slow RUMBLE begins to grow underneath the building. "What the?" He moves to the bay window looking out over the tracks. The track is right below.

A freight train APPROACHES. Its light glares right into the room. Blinding him! Its whistle BLOWS. Vincent is FREAKED! It looks like the train is charging right through his room.

He stumbles back and over to the bed, holding on.

The entire building HEAVES and SHAKES while the train NEARS, PASSES, and DRIFTS into the distance. It's like experiencing a long drawn out earthquake.

He sits there gripping his bed, his door having drifted open from the shaking.

Quinnly is watching him. Both amused and drunk. Her drink in one hand. Unlit cig in the other. Clad in a flimsy damp nightgown. Dripping from getting out of the bath.

QUINNLY
Always come out here case this tongue depressant finally decides to collapse.
(steps into the room)

VINCENT
Mon Dieu, my heart she... the tracks run --

QUINNLY
-- Yeah, dumb huh? Something to do with some old Chinamen mathematician a long-long time ago and that dried up river gorge over there. Come fall it'll have water in it again I hear.

VINCENT
Who'd put a building in such...?

QUINNLY
Was here first.
(moves further into the room)
This whole stinkin' town's been here for about forever. You ever hear of this dang place? Way out lost... all this lunacy. Have ya?

VINCENT
No.

QUINNLY
Nobody has, far as I know. Wasn't even listed on the train stops.

VINCENT
The people who gave me a lift knew.

QUINNLY
You notice they ain't with you. So, the question is, you got a match?

VINCENT
I do, actually.

She leans down to him. Giving him the eye. And a look down her gown. Still dripping on the floor. He lights her cig. She takes the match and lights the candle. She steps back, looking about his room.

QUINNLY
You travel light.

VINCENT
Drove my rental into a river, two states back. Came close to drowning.

QUINNLY
Congratulations. You made it to this inbred shithole. You look like one of them urban cowpokes in that getup.

VINCENT
It was between this and a Levi evening gown. And my knees are all skinned.

QUINNLY
What do you know, a sense of humor. What do they call that... self defecating?

VINCENT
Apparently.

QUINNLY
I bet you're married with kids, even.

VINCENT
Oui, Mon Sheri, our first on the way. A boy we hope.

Vincent hands a wet PHOTO to Quinnly. She looks at it, smiles.

QUINNLY
Your wife's American, and real pretty. I bet your kid will be as cute as a puppy.

VINCENT
Points for not sounding surprised.

QUINNLY
She must be worried sick. Hubby stuck way out here all by his lonesome.

VINCENT
Oui, I rang ahead. I didn't explain all this. She knows I'm delayed but on my way.

QUINNLY
Business or pleasure?

VINCENT
Neither. It seems I'm a washed-up suit peddler. Soon to be lost of my job when my father finds how badly I've failed him.

QUINNLY
What kind of suits?

VINCENT
Business suits. Haute couture. The finest, from my family's boutique de tailleur in Paris. Completely hand stitched by my aunts and uncles. But all --

QUINNLY
-- back there in your rental?

VINCENT
Oui. Our entire sample line, disparu - vanished. Stolen by the river. Incroyable... terrible. I've missed every appointment. It's a catastrophe, no? And my family... how do I tell them I've failed so miserably?

Quinnly sits beside Vincent. Lots of leg causing uncomfortable silence. He looks to the hall, expecting an angry Sheriff at any second. Least he should screw up again.

VINCENT
Maybe you should....

QUINNLY
So, you're out to save your family's business, Captain Frenchy?

VINCENT
Not quite. I was to launch our line, from New York to Salt Lake on my way. What a disaster. My poor father --

QUINNLY
-- is against you being here? Now this.

VINCENT
Oui. My Sheri inherited a lovely home in Salt Lake City. There is family debt, from her mother's mental illness, and we have a little one coming. So, she is... somewhat stuck. I was on my way... first sailing the ocean... and then crossing America to be with her.

QUINNLY
Not exactly gay Paris, last I read.

VINCENT
No. She is arrived just three months. Her mother, she is in a nursing home, so I... No matter, I am on my way with my tail between my legs. I am... such a loser, no?

Quinnly moves to the bathroom. Drops her cig in the toilet. Adds water to her drink. Comes out. Lights another cig on the candle. She blows the smoke at Vincent as he gets up open the hall door. Checking the hallway.

QUINNLY
Sorry. You're only a loser if you stop trying. Like my boy toy Roy who got the dumb idea to get off the tracks. We won one of them train passes where we could just come and go. Like a free ticket to Never-Never Land.

She moves over to the window. Looks up and down the track. Dragging hard, saddened.

QUINNLY
Only never means never, so you never really get there. Turns out the loser did just that. Cum and went for another bottle of rye. And never came back to get me out of this place.

VINCENT
I'm sorry....

QUINNLY
Don't be, there's a moral to this story somewhere. I got an angry mouth when I drink.
(moves to him, very close)
But you know, you're the first in a long time I ain't got sore at. And I've had plenty already.

VINCENT
Maybe you ought to slow down.

QUINNLY
Don't push your luck. It's probably because you don't want things from me. I don't get that much. You're kind'a cute when you quiver like this.

VINCENT
Oui, well... that sheriff friend of yours, seemed adamant about me staying out of trouble.

QUINNLY
So, being like this... close... is --

VINCENT
-- This? This is... big time trouble.

**Lights Up on Driftwood Lobby - Continuing**

Dane enters with a bottle or Rye. Stops. Goes to the counter. Opens the registry, checking guest list. Looks up at the sound of Quinnly's voice.

**Lights Black on Driftwood Lobby**

QUINNLY
I'm about to go crackers. You know? This place. If I was you, I wouldn't wait for no train. I'd get out of here first light in the morning. If not sooner. This town's not mentally sound by plenty.

VINCENT
Merci, I've been thinking just these things.

Quinnly looks at him real close. Examining his features. Searching every inch of it. She's so close her breath is on his face letting him smell her liquor.

QUINNLY
You smell clean. You even sound clean. I ain't known clean since I been here. This filthy dustbowl. Nothing but inbred pig and chicken rancher stink.

She kisses him. Hard. Pressing her body up against him. Feeling him, all over. He struggles to get away. She pulls back just as quick. Taking his breath away. She backs away. He tries hard to compose himself, checking the staircase.

QUINNLY
Always the losers, never the nice guys.

VINCENT
Maybe you should just flee this place.

QUINNLY
Your wife's a lucky woman, I might, you invite me.

Dane stops in the open door with the bottle of rye.

DANE
What is this?

QUINNLY
It ain't nothing. We're just talking about shit you ain't got the wit for.

DANE
You don't need to be talkin' shit with every drifter who comes through this town.

QUINNLY
He's not a drifter. He's a fine suit salesman.

VINCENT
Qui, and happily married. Very happy.
(displays the evidence)

DANE
I'd be in a mighty big hurry to get back to her.

VINCENT
I'm on the road at sunrise. If not sooner.

DANE
That's the smartest damn thing I heard coming out of this room.

QUINNLY
Leave him alone.

DANE
You watch your mouth, girl.

QUINNLY
Or what? You gonna get all mean and ugly on me like your fat old Deputy-Do-Reilly?

DANE
I just might. If I have to.

QUINNLY
Shit, I'd wet my panties if I had some on.
(drops her cig to the floor and steps on it with her barefoot, blowing the smoke at Dane)
I'd bob you so close we'd look like twins. Move it.
(pushes past Dane)
And give me that.
(snatches bottle, twists top)
You take all night getting back here, I'll talk to who the hell I want.
(pulls from the bottle, leaves)

DANE
(shows his gun)
Last warning... don't be startin' no trouble, Frenchy.

**Lights Black on Vincent's Rooms**

**End of ACT I**
**Scene Four**

**ACT I**
**Scene Five**

**Lights Up on Lobby/Poolhall/Bar**

Vincent finds the Lobby dimly lit. Two figures step out of the shadows. Travis and Leonardo.

TRAVIS
Café just about closed.

LEONARDO
You want something else, you might find it behind the bar.

VINCENT
Merci, perhaps... just a place to sit and think.

TRAVIS
It's your Friday night.

The two men head toward the bar. The DRONE of a small airplane APPROACHING for landing GROANS overhead.

Vincent heads for the front door, attempting to leave the lobby into the street. He turns to look up at the plane and finds Travis standing right behind him.

TRAVIS
Wouldn't be neighborly like to let you stand out here in the dust, now would it.

VINCENT
Listen, I... is there an airport?

TRAVIS
Nah, probably just them crop dusters the famers got.

Leonardo stops at bar/poolhall door, wanting to go in.

LEONARDO
(playing along)
-- Yeah, sure, all it is.

TRAVIS
Come on, we'll buy ya a beer. Hey, Leonardo, we got enough to buy our foreign friend a good American beer?

LEONARDO
We'll be winning at the table soon enough.

VINCENT
No please, I have --

TRAVIS
-- Good, you got cash... you spot us the first round and we'll take it from there.

VINCENT
You're too kind, but considering --

LEONARDO
-- We goin' in, or what?

Travis is all but dragging Vincent across the Lobby into the poolhall/bar.

TRAVIS
Hold on to your pecker, Leonardo. Our froggy friend here offered to stake us a round.

LEONARDO
(opens the poolhall's door)
Then get your asses on over. Table's about to free up.

**Black on Lobby**

**Lights Up on Poolhall/Bar - Continuing**

Leonardo has made his way to a pool table in the center of the smoky room.

Jeremiad, the small-time lawyer and the best looking girl in the room, ISABEL, are there. He has the table as he finishes up a game.

Eli, the odd looking little chicken rancher, pays up.

Brooke is waiting on tables. Deputy Tomcat Reilly is at the bar drinking next to Zachary.

A JUKEBOX in B.G. Travis pushes Vincent to the bar, brushing up against Reilly.

REILLY

Hey, what's the rush?

VINCENT

Pardon --

REILLY

(broadly mocking accent)

-- Pardon... ain't gonna cut it you step on my hides again.

ZACHARY

(leans in on Reilly)

Don't be giving Frenchy here any of your deputy-do-shit, Reilly. Boy's a guest in our fine country.

Reilly looks Zachary over and turns away to the Stationmaster.

REILLY

Let anybody in this place.

BARTENDER

Let you in, didn't I?

The three of them think it's funny. Vincent looks around and is greeted with a knowing nod by both Zachary and the Stationmaster.

Travis flags down the BARTENDER, 40's, missing an arm and an eye.

TRAVIS

Three cold ones.

BARTENDER
Let's see some money.

Travis pulls Vincent near.

TRAVIS
Why don't we start a tab?

Vincent reluctantly takes out his money and pays instead.

TRAVIS
How'd you like to redouble that dough?

VINCENT
Generous, but....

Quinnly, very drunk, enters the poolhall bar with Truly. They make their way over to a table near the pool table. Travis takes all three beers and works his way over to the pool table and hands one to Leonardo.

LEONARDO
Shit, would ya looky there. Just like clockwork.

TRAVIS
Don't go buck-crazy on me now.

LEONARDO
I'm thinkin' I'm gonna lick me some salt tonight.

TRAVIS
And I'm thinkin' I don't want to kick some redneck stupid.

LEONARDO
How much our little friend holdin'?

TRAVIS
Close to two C's.

LEONARDO
He in?

TRAVIS
Does he get a choice?

Vincent stands at the bar wanting to leave real bad. He heads toward the door. But when he gets there an unlit cigarette is thrust in his face.

QUINNLY
Still got them matches?

Vincent finds Quinnly against him. Her breath stale from booze and smoke... steadying herself on his arm.

QUINNLY
Couldn't sleep?

VINCENT
Restless night.

QUINNLY
There's local pig links behind the bar. Not bad, you catch them early.
(puts her cig to her lips)
You gonna light me?

Vincent lights her cig.

QUINNLY
You ain't leavin'?

VINCENT
I was thinking....

QUINNLY
Oh, come on... I just got here. You can't leave me with all these organ donors to gas to. It wouldn't be gentlemanly of you.

LEONARDO
(racking the balls)
How about we play ten a ball?

JEREMIAD
What do you say we count your friend's money first.

Quinnly uses Vincent to steady herself to the table where Truly already has drinks waiting for them.

Travis looks over and sees them sitting. He goes over to Vincent and leans down close to him.

TRAVIS
Pull it out and put it on the table. Man wants to see how big our dicks are.

VINCENT
Pardonnez-moi?

QUINNLY
He means your money.

TRAVIS
Hurry up.

VINCENT
I think not....

QUINNLY
(puts her hand on Vincent's)
It's okay. I've seen these two play. You'll get your money back and some.
(pulls Travis close by shirt)
You cheat Vincent. I hurt you.

TRAVIS
That a promise?

Quinnly lets Travis go.

VINCENT
(takes out money)
Where's my beer?

TRAVIS
Order another, Leonardo was thirsty. Make it three, and whatever the girls want.

Travis goes back to the pool table and Jeremiad.

TRAVIS
You satisfied?

JEREMIAD
(looks Vincent over)
Alright, closest ball.

Leonardo takes a ball and pushes it with a cue stick right up against the far bank. Jeremiad does the same but his ball bounces back.

While Leonardo breaks and runs the table.

QUINNLY
(sees Vincent's face)
Relax.... The tall one there, he ain't much but he can dance. And the dim one, he's the player. Met them over at a dance hall down the road.

Truly leans over to Quinnly.

TRULY
I think he likes me.

QUINNLY
Which one?

TRULY
Him.

From across the table Leonardo looks past his stick at Truly. He grins.

TRULY
Oh good, I'm gonna get manned tonight.

VINCENT
Where's your Sheriff friend?

QUINNLY
Screw him. Probably squealin' pigs.

She puts her hand in Vincent's lap.

VINCENT
I need to get some air.

QUINNLY
Hold on, you're about to double your money.

Leonardo sinks the last ball.

JEREMIAD
What the hell was that?

TRAVIS
I'll show you again if you wanna play double or nothin'?

JEREMIAD
You guys professional?

TRAVIS
We look professional to you?

LEONARDO
I'm just in a good mood. You want another go, it's double.

Vincent turns to the drinkers crowding the bar. Eli smiling a toothless grin. He gives Vincent a look on his way to the restroom. Vincent looks away seeing Eli vetting him.

JEREMIAD
I'm being set up here, ain't I.

STATIONMASTER
Be about time someone took our hard earned currency back from you, J.J.

ZACHARY
Got a hundred on the dumb looking one.

BARTENDER
And which one might that be? The lawyer or the grifter?

STATIONMASTER
Shit. Which one's the grifter?

Jeremiad gives the laughing crowd a hard look. He turns back to Leonardo.

JEREMIAD
Alright, but this game ain't over 'till I say it's over.

Jeremiad takes out more of his money. Puts it on the table. Vincent tries to pick his up. Jeremiad pins his hand to the table with a cue stick.

JEREMIAD
I'll let you know when to pick the money up, mister.

BROOKE
You need anything?

Quinnly sees makeup over Brooke's shiner, then looks at Reilly, who gives her a smug look. Quinnly flips him off as he heads to the bathrooms.

QUINNLY
Why don't you come spend the night with me, Brooke?

BROOKE
Dane would love that.

QUINNLY
Shit, kick his ass to the floor. Pig wouldn't even notice.

BROOKE
I just might, at that.

TRULY
Enough with the butch shit, you two. Give us all beers.

Brooke sticks out her tongue, hiking her ass as she walks towards the bar. Vincent leans into Quinnly who's watching Brooke.

VINCENT
I must relieve myself. Which way?

QUINNLY
Straight back. Don't get lost.

Vincent makes his way to the bathroom finding himself at the back door. The bathroom door opens.

ELI
Come on in, four-eyes. I've been expecting you.

VINCENT
Oh, damn....

The back door opens. Reilly enters zipping up his pants. Vincent makes it out the door.

**Black on Poolhall/Bar**

**Lights Up on Alley - Continuing**

Rear of Poolhall/Café - Night. Single light over the door. As the door closes, Vincent looks for a place to pee... when Dane's MUFFLED VOICE makes him look.

Dane carries two money bags into the dark and O.S.

Vincent ducks behind garbage cans.

Suddenly, Cheryl and Blair, BURST out the Café's backdoor, hot for each other. He pins her against the wall.

BLAIR
Oh shit, Cheryl, I'm gonna knock you up right here.

CHERYL
Not again, you ain't. Take me to the truck.

BLAIR
Shit, we don't need....
(looks down)
What the hell you doin' there?

CHERYL
Oh, my god, put my dress down, Blair.

BLAIR
I said....

CHERYL
The freak can see my panties.

VINCENT
I just needed fresh air.

BLAIR
Well you ain't gettin' any sniffin' around down there.

Vincent gets up, looking in Dane's direction. Blair follows his eyes.

BLAIR
Don't make me tell you again, boy.

VINCENT
Believe me....
(runs O.S.)

CHERYL
You let that shit see my ass.

BLAIR
(looks after Vincent, running his hand back under her dress)
Hell, you probably liked it.

**Black on Alley**

**Lights Up on Cross Road - Continuing**

Vincent makes his way around the last building. Finds himself back where he started. Takes a pee.

O.S., a TRUCK leaves town. Vincent hurries to finish up. Arms in the air... realizing it's Eli's truck... searches for a place to hide. Nothing.

The chicken truck SCREECHES to a stop O.S. Eli gets out with a bang of his door and enters stage.

ELI
Why, looky here. Hey there, four-eyes. I hunted all over back there. Funny guy, out here waving your dill pickle when the poolhall's got a perfectly good indoor crapper.

VINCENT
Well I, I was leaving town and....

ELI
Shit dang, you're in lots of luck. I reside but a spit up the road.

VINCENT
Oh... man....

ELI
Yeah, takes some gettin' use to. Place ain't much to look at but it's upwind to the coops and I got a hide-a-bed my hounds sleep on. Get you a bite of down home American late night vitals. You like possum stew? Home baked biscuits? Some greens. Sounds good. Don't it?

VINCENT
No... it's....

ELI
Eli. I seen you looking all shy. I ain't queer or nothin'... it's just the damn girls in these parts don't go for me.

VINCENT
Well actually, Eli, it's just... I'll wait for a longer ride.

ELI
You sure? Not much traffic through these parts on the weekend. Could use the company. Vincent was your name?

VINCENT
I'm not interested.

ELI
Nobody's gonna say....

VINCENT
(picks up a rock)
Look, I clearly stated I'm not interested. Now leave me alone.

ELI
Dang, ain't you somethin' when you get all riled up. I got television reception. Even got dirty photos of local gals. You don't have to touch me. Doc says stimulation's good for --

Vincent throws the rock. The chickens to THRASH. Alarmed, Eli runs O.S and peals out of there. Feathers floating.

VINCENT
Bonjour, egg man.

**Black on Crossroads**

**Lights Up on Pool Hall/Bar - Continuing**

Int. Pool Hall/Bar - Night. Quinnly enters from the alley to find Jeremiad out cold on the bar floor. Travis stands over him with a cue stick.

TRAVIS
Damn it, Leonardo. See what you made me go and do? Damn it, I hate this kind of senseless violence.

Leonardo picks up the money. Quinnly stops him.

QUINNLY
Vincent's?

Leonardo throws a wad of bills on the table, as Travis joins him in backing out. Reilly and Blair step in their way at the door.

REILLY
Wouldn't be nice to leave it this way.

TRAVIS
You saw it, was an intervention. I might've saved that man's life.

TRULY
(comes up behind them)
Get out of the way, Reilly. How many times you whacked J.J. yourself over that table?

Reilly and Blair back off. Leonardo, Travis, and Truly exit.

QUINNLY
(puts Vincent's money in bra)
Better get him some attention.

ZACHARY
He's a lawyer, how much could he bleed?

**Black on Poolhall/Bar**

**End of ACT I**
**Scene Five**

**ACT II**
**Scene One**

**Lights Up on Spoon Café**

Vincent enters the Spoon Café - Daybreak, making sure the screen door doesn't slap. He looks like crap.

The place is busy compared to yesterday. Note: May use crewmembers as town folks.

Quinnly works the counter and Cheryl waits tables.

The Stationmaster and Zachary sit at a booth. Dane is at another table with Jeremiad.

Vincent looks around. Tables are all full. He goes over and sits at the counter.

Blair fry-cooks on the other side of the order window.

Quinnly turns from buttering toast to find Vincent. She looks past him at Dane and Jeremiad who are looking back.

Vincent goes through his pockets and pulls out a handful of change. Puts it on the counter.

VINCENT

Coffee.

Quinnly pours him some. She takes the wad of bills out of her bra and tosses it on the counter.

VINCENT

Merci.

QUINNLY

Thought you run off?

VINCENT

(glances to find Dane looking)

Minor complications.

QUINNLY

I came to your room.

VINCENT
I was on the road praying for a ride.

QUINNLY
Guess you ain't got the thumb for it.

VINCENT
Helps if someone actually passes by.

CHERYL
(hangs a ticket in the order window)
Two specials, one up, one easy. Ham on both.
(gives Vincent a hard look)
Ain't seen enough?

QUINNLY
(hands her the toast)
Take this to Zachary.

Cheryl takes the toast and walks away with a fresh pot of coffee.

Quinnly gives Vincent a look. He gives her one back.

QUINNLY
You missed a good time.

VINCENT
Not by much.

QUINNLY
You sore at me?

VINCENT
No. Frustrated. Eggs easy. Short stack. Maple if you please. And jus d'orange.

Quinnly, miffed by his attitude. Hangs the order in the window. Blair takes the ticket, sees Vincent.

BLAIR
Hey, I thought I told you --

QUINNLY
-- Shut up, Blair... you're a lousy fry cook, with kids, in a dry bed shithole, get over it.

BLAIR
The guy was creeping around --

QUINNLY
-- Who'd know better, than you two ally cats?

BLAIR
I don't need no smart mouth....
(sees Dane stand up)
I'm just saying, is all.

A distant train whistle blows. Dane moves up behind Vincent, counting his money. Jeremiad leaves. Blair goes back to work.

DANE
I was told you left town, Frenchy?

VINCENT
Tried. But no one offered, except the egg man.

DANE
(drops money on the counter)
Probably just wantin' company.

QUINNLY
(takes the money and rings)
Maybe he got it.

Dane tips quarters. Sits next to Vincent.

DANE
Friendlier farm traffic up on the back road to Clear Water. Might even hop a train.

VINCENT
Hate to see the back road if --

DANE
-- Safer up there too.

Quinnly nods her head. Giving Vincent assuring look.

VINCENT
Well, I --

DANE
-- Eat up. I'll walk you on up that way.

**Lights to Black on Café**

**Lights Up on Dane and Vincent**

Dane and Vincent walk north out of town - Morning.

Dane takes out a cigar as they walk. Looks over at Vincent. Vincent looks ready to run. Dane unhooks his work revolver and hands it to Vincent. Nice. Shinny. He now can reach into his pocket for the lighter. Scratches his balls while he's there.

Vincent just looks at the revolver, confused. Dane reaches into his pocket again. Takes out shells, hands them to Vincent.

DANE

Load that, will ya.

Vincent can't believe what he's hearing. He hesitantly takes the bullets.

DANE

You ever use one?

VINCENT

Not yet.

Dane smiles. Vincent loads the gun. They stop at a railroad crossing sign at the track just outside of town.

A TRAIN is approaching in the near distance. Ground starts shaking. Dane looks at Vincent. Vincent still has the revolver. Dane waits. Still with the cigar. Vincent is making up his mind. Vincent finally hands Dane back the gun. With no place to hide.

DANE

Trains slow-down to change tracks before passing through the mountains. Hobos leave the boxcars open for each other. The ones on this track move pretty fast. Just follow this road about ten miles. There'll be at least four more before nightfall. You'll catch one.

Vincent backs away. Dane checks his gun to see if Vincent actually loaded it. Dane smiles at Vincent. The train starts SOUNDING its horn.

DANE
(having to yell)
You a God fearing boy, Frenchy?

VINCENT
(yelling back)
Are you?

Dane aims toward Vincent. Vincent walks backward trying to beat the TRAIN to get across the tracks.

Dane FIRES. The railroad crossing sign CLANGS with each shot just beyond Vincent's head. Vincent stands there in shock as the sign WIGGLES.

DANE
New sign.

The TRAIN blasts by between them, the shadow and broken light flickering on his Vincent's face.

**Lights to Black on Vincent**

**End of ACT II**
**Scene One**

**ACT II**
**Scene Two**

**Lights Up on Ext. Spoon Café**

Driftwood Crossing - Noon. A TRAIN in the distance again.

QUINNLY comes out of the FLOPHOUSE where Reilly sits on the stoop. His brimmed hat down over his eyes, snoring. She has changed clothes, holds onto a post for support as the building begins to shake.

The TRAIN is coming on quick. Shaking the Flophouse harder. Jeremiad steps out of the Flophouse with his que stick. Flings a SPIT of chew out into the street. Reacts to the disgusted looks on Quinnly's face. He checks his watch. Hangs on to the other post.

DANE comes out of the Cafe'. He takes out a handful of shells and reloads his revolver.

Quinnly stops beside Dane. She looks over at Reilly to make sure he can't hear under the APPROACHING train.

QUINNLY

Any sign of them?

DANE

I'm assumin' they tell time.

QUINNLY

What about J.J.?

DANE

Train hits, he goes back in. They know.

Travis and Leonardo come strolling out of the flophouse feeling good.

LEONARDO

What did I tell you about that girl?

Travis takes in the town. Looks down at sleeping Reilly. And over to Dane and Quinnly.

TRAVIS

Enjoyed being tied and gagged, too.

Dane holds up two fingers. Travis nods and heads... across the road toward the O.S. bank. Leonardo follows.

**Lights Black on Town**

**Lights Up on Int. Bank - Continuing**

The building VIBRATES.

Isabel is at a desk behind the counter counting money.

Cheryl has finished her deposit and is leaving. Travis and Leonardo suddenly squeeze past Cheryl as she pushes the door open. Leonardo covers the door.

Isabel looks up to find Travis leaping the counter with a gun pointed at her.

TRAVIS

Don't bother.

ISABEL

I knew you was no good.

LEONARDO

(moves to the window)

Grab them up, let's go. We got unexpected people gathering out here.

TRAVIS

Open up!

Isabel moves to a gate blocking the safe and pulls the door open. Inside are ten full money bags.

The TRAIN is nearly on the town... very intense. Everything RATTLES and SHAKES. They all have to yell.

TRAVIS

Which ones got the most?

(grabs Isabel)

LEONARDO

Shit this ain't good. We got that chicken truck pullin' up outside. It's got our car blocked in. Dammit, he's gettin' out. The cook from the café and kids, pickin' up his wife, are blocked in, too.

TRAVIS

Which bags?!

ISABEL

They're tagged.

Travis pushes her down to the floor of the safe. He checks some of the bags, grabs two.

TRAVIS

Stay right there.

LEONARDO

We got the two from the café. The Sheriff and Quinnly across the street. Lawyer standing outside. The deputy supposed be watchin' the place, is still sunning himself, but waking up. And that truck's still got us blocked. Fuck! He's givin' the kids painted eggs.

Train is getting closer. Everything shaking is making everything chaotic.

Travis jumps back over the counter. Stops at the window with Leonardo. He hands him a bag.

TRAVIS
Let's go. We're right on time.

LEONARDO
You heard what I said?

TRAVIS
We'll make him move.

The Train hits the town.

**Lights to Black on Inside Bank**

**Lights Up on Driftwood Crossing - Continue**

Ext. Driftwood - Minutes Later - THERE'S BEEN A SHOOTOUT.

The train has passed moving west. Brooke hold's Reilly. See's he's been shot in the back by his blood in her hand. He's sobbing. She softly laughs, closes his eyes.

BROOKE
You fat bastard, Reilly. Can't even die like a man.

Quinnly is crunched down inside the Lobby door of the of the Flophouse, as Dane reloads his gun.

QUINNLY
You moron, I thought you had this all worked out.

DANE
There's only two gallons of gas in that convertible.

QUINNLY
Well we're screwed now. They ain't in it.

DANE
Don't matter which direction they go. I'll find them by the stink of that chicken truck.

QUINNLY
You didn't mention shooting Reilly.

DANE

Keeps it simple, don't it.

He takes another GUN from his pocket. Gives Quinnly a hard look. She takes it from him.

DANE

Stay down.

Zachary, Jeremiad, and Blair enter stage with their guns drawn. The Stationmaster stands alone shaking his head at the mess.

Eli is crazily crying, crawling on his knees picking up his chicken cages, trying to save his chickens.

ZACHARY

Ain't you goin' after them?

Dane watches Eli in the street. Eli stands. Bleeding chicken in both hands. The Stationmaster locks eyes with Dane. He knows something isn't right.

DANE

Of course I'm goin' after them. Give me a minute to think this out. Blair, shut him up.

ZACHARY

There ain't no rules saying you have to give them a head start.

JEREMIAD

We're goin' with you.

DANE

No, ya ain't.

JEREMIAD

They killed Reilly, for Christ's sakes.

BLAIR

We can't just let them go.

DANE

We ain't, Blair. Now, shut him up.

Blair moves to Eli, takes a hold, pulls him close. Eli sobbing, holding bloody chickens.

DANE
J.J., I want you all here for the bank truck, as usual. Eli, don't make me hurt you.

Blair takes Eli out of the road. Isabel and Cheryl go to Brooke and Reilly. The Stationmaster looks at Reilly. Thinking. Then over to Dane. Checks his pocket watch.

DANE
You got something to add, old man?

STATIONMASTER
Nothin' worth adding. Time I call in the spirits, is all.
(goes inside the train station)

DANE
Get Reilly off the sidewalk. And clean this fucking mess up.

ZACHARY
What do you want us to tell the bank people?

DANE
Tell them the truth. I'm out on business.

JEREMIAD
We ain't gonna tell them?

DANE
You want the Feds poking their heads around here, J.J.? Any of you?

ZACHARY
I reckon you're right on that.

DANE
This is between us. I'll square it with Tony and Davis after they fly in Monday. Isabel, you get on that bank wire and adjust what you think they took.

A sudden GUNSHOT O.S. from inside the train station as Dane goes back for Quinnly. The others run toward it.

QUINNLY
This better work.

DANE
You want out? Get out.

QUINNLY
Screw it. Let's find them, take our money... and get the hell out of this stinkin' place.

DANE
We'll probably have to kill them now.

QUINNLY
You'll have to catch them first.

**Black on Driftwood Crossing**

**End of ACT II**
**Scene Two**

**ACT II**
**Scene Three**

**Lights Up on Open Boxcar**

Ext./Int. moving Open-Boxcar - Train - Day. Travis gets a death grip on the railing. Swings the second money bag onto the boxcar floor. Nearly floating to climb in.

O.S. Dane FIRES and... STRIKES Travis in the back, actually helping him, pushing him toward the door. A sickening OUTCRY.

TRAVIS
Oh, sweet Mary, find me a way.

Dane FIRES O.S.... Travis... feet DRAGGING in the gravel, is STRUCK in the leg.

Travis loses strength to hang on.

But instead of falling off... he is ABRUPTLY dragged onto the train by Vincent as he reaches out from the boxcar and grabs Travis' wrist.

Vincent looks out of the boxcar to see Dane.

**Lights Black on Vincent and Boxcar**

**Lights Up on Dane/Quinnly/Leonardo in Field**

Quinnly sits in the dirt. Leonardo is dead beside her.

Dane runs past them, not noticing. Completely frustrated. Racking his brain on how to fix this mess.

DANE

That son-of-a-bitch.

Quinnly eyes blinking weakly. Life slipping from her.

DANE

Shit. Frenchy's got both bags....

(figures it out)

Come on, get off your ass...

(heads for the truck)

...we'll catch'em at the overpass when the train....

He looks back. Seeing Quinnly from upstage. Walks downstage and around her to see ...

...Quinnly's blood slowly pumps onto her lap from a bad neck wound. Her gun on him.

DANE

Jesus Christ!

QUINNLY

Let him go home to his pretty pregnant wife.

DANE

He's got our fucking money.

Quinnly pulls the trigger, it clicks empty.

Dane leans down, takes his gun back and watches her blood spill out as he thinks of what to do next.

Slowly she gets weaker. A dribble. There's more pain in his eyes than hers.

QUINNLY

I know you killed my Roy Toy so you could play with me. You dumb bastared... you ain't even got the money.

Quinnly dies. Falls sideways into the dirt.

**Black on Dane in Field**

**Lights up on Vincent and Travis in Moving Boxcar**

Int. open Boxcar - Day. Vincent has pulled Travis in and drags him to the other side of the boxcar, leaning him sitting upright. Travis bleeds where the bullet passed through him. Vincent pulls money out of a bag. Trying to stop the bleeding.

TRAVIS

Thanks... it's a waste.

(grabs Vincent's hand)

Stop, Frenchy.

VINCENT

But I can --

TRAVIS

-- It's over. I'm done for.

VINCENT

How far to the next stop?

Travis shakes his head. Vincent looks out of the boxcar, then back at the bags. Makes up his mind. Picks them up. He looks at the open boxcar door. He draws back with one to throw it out.

Travis manages to point his gun and fire, hitting just to the right of Vincent's head. Vincent ducks.

TRAVIS

Drop the bags.

Vincent drops the bags. He turns to find Travis fighting to keep the gun on him.

VINCENT

This can't be good money, Travis.

TRAVIS

Laundered. Cincinnati Mob.

VINCENT
If we give it back, he'll let us go. No?

TRAVIS
You got family, right?

VINCENT
My wife is with baby. But --

TRAVIS
-- Get a clear picture. When we get into the mountains. Jump with the money.

VINCENT
But I don't want this. I just want to go home.

TRAVIS
With or without... you're a loose end to an inside robbery and murder. Don't give him this money....

Travis passes out from the pain. Vincent crawls to the open door and looks out. Not sure what to do next.

Vincent reaches for the moneybags again. This time dragging them crossing the open door.

O.S. from the overpass, Dane starts SHOOTING at the moving train.

Vincent scrambles for cover. Dane's bullets rip through the wood boxcar.

Vincent scurries over to Travis and takes his gun out of his hand. Checks for a pulse. Who knows?

He looks to see how many bullets. One. He searches Travis's pocket's finding no other shells.

The SHOOTING finally stops, and Vincent looks out a bullet hole in the boxcar wall.

A hard heavy jerk rocks the train as it slows down, climbing mountains.

Vincent looks outside at the growing steep terrain. He turns back to find the jerking has brought Travis back around. He's weaker.

VINCENT
The train's slowing down.

TRAVIS
Climbin'. Careful, he can get on up here if he made it to the overpass.

VINCENT
Shit... you and Leonardo, what would you have done?

TRAVIS
Leap Clear Water Bridge. Three hun'... feet. Camps... we left a truck parked. Take this.
(holds out key)

VINCENT
(doesn't take it)
Three... but that's insane.

TRAVIS
Yeah, backup 'case things went south. You'll make it... if you swim good. Take the key.

Vincent can't swim at all.

TRAVIS
All this money... and you.... Not a lick?

VINCENT
Oui, I was this close to drowning just yesterday. I'm in no big hurry to try again.

TRAVIS
It's coming up quick. Better fix your sights. Take this....

Travis feels for his gun. Vincent shows it.

VINCENT
But... Christ, there must be police in the next town.

TRAVIS
That won't stop them. Who knows who they own out here.

Vincent isn't sure. He doesn't have much time to think it out... because the bridge is coming up fast. He watches out the door. The ground drops off steep.

Vincent, near panic, grabs the bags. He wraps his gun and glasses his jacket. He takes out the picture and kisses it. Putting it all into the bag.

He grabs the key from Travis. And looks outside, then back at Travis. Picks the bags up. It's obvious, there's no way he'd ever jump.

There's a sudden big thump from up above.

TRAVIS

Jump, Frenchy jump!

VINCENT

I can't!

Dane swings into the boxcar from the other side.

Vincent stumbles back. Having to grab the side of the door to keep from falling out with a heavy bag in each hand.

Travis tries to stab Dane in the foot. Making Dane stumble as he runs at Vincent, grabbing at the bags.

Causing Dane to push Vincent further out the door.

Only this time the weight of the bags make Vincent teeter backwards. He fights to keep from falling out.

Dane reaches for him again. Grabbing his shirt.

The train enters under the bridge trestles. Vincent is beyond fighting to regain balance but has good footing.

Dane can't hold him up, being jerked by the train. He could get pulled out. So he let's go.

TRAVIS

Do it!

Out of sheer panic, Vincent leaps with all his might backwards. Just missing the first bridge trestle.

O.S., Vincent's FADING SCREAM echos as he falls three hundred feet down to the rapids below.

Dane moves to the door. He couldn't jump if he had the balls to because of the bridge trestles. He watches below trying to see Vincent.

Whistle BLOWING, the train takes Dane into the mountains. Just before it takes him out of view of the river. He sees something.

TRAVIS

Made it, didn't he.

DANE

Not yet.

Smile grows on Travis' face as he dies.

**Black on Open Boxcar**

**End of ACT II**
**Scene Three**

**ACT II**
**Scene Four**

**Lights Up on Driftwood Whistle Inn**

Int. Driftwood Whistle Lobby - Night. Under noise from the Poolhall/bar.

Dane is at the front desk, rips out the page Vincent signed. But can't read it in the dark. He reaches to turn on the desk light and finds Jeremiad Johnstone with a gun.

JEREMIAD

Keep the lights off. Put your hands where I can see them.

DANE

You couldn't find a game, J.J?

JEREMIAD

You dumb pig fucker. What'd you go and do?

DANE

I caught up with them and killed them. Like I said I'd do. Why?

JEREMIAD

I found Quinnly. You kill her, too?

DANE
What do you think?

JEREMIAD
I found both your suitcases in the truck, is what I think.

DANE
Where is my truck?

JEREMIAD
Where's the money?

DANE
That's it? You want in?

JEREMIAD
No. I want you out.

DANE
What'd you tell Cincinnati?

JEREMIAD
I just told 'em I was taken over, because you were dead.

DANE
That's how it is?

JEREMIAD
You got a better way out of this mess?

DANE
(quick draws, killing J.J.)
Matter of fact I do.

**Black on Driftwood Inn**

**End of ACT II**
**Scene Four**

**ACT II**
**Scene Five**

**Lights Up on Phonebooth**

Vincent stands down the road from his home in the lonely roadside phonebooth - Daybreak. He's got a broken leg held together with sticks and his Levi shirt sleaves.

Phone RINGING on the other end.

SHERI (V.O.)
Hello?

VINCENT
Did he hurt you?

SHERI ( V.O)
Non.

VINCENT
I am near, you understand? Let me talk to the Sheriff.

SHERI (V.O.)
Oui. He wants to speak with you.

DANE (V.O.)
So you made it. Good for you, Frenchy?

VINCENT
Sheriff.... You will fail to find what you are after if you harm my family. If you want it, use a payphone at the gas station on Main and Walker. I will call you there.

DANE (V.O.)
Sorry, it doesn't work that way. You tell me right now or I start on your wife and the baby she's carrying. You got two seconds. One, two --

VINCENT
-- Wait, I'll tell you. But --

DANE (V.O.)
-- But nothin'. Just tell me. It's your only choice.

VINCENT
Okay. There's a campsite about a half-mile back from where I jumped called Jokers Point.

DANE (V.O.)
Okay. I know it.

VINCENT
Look for a large rotting oak tree just to the north before the trestle starts above. About a hundred yards off the river. There's a rock against its base. You can't miss it. Move the rock and dig between the two thickest roots. Everything is there.

DANE (V.O.)
You better not be lyin'.

VINCENT
Just let me come home. That's all I want from this.

DANE (V.O.)
Let me think it over.

VINCENT
Please, I'm begging you. I only want my wife and child safe. To be with her. That's all I ever wanted. Just to reach home. Not the money. I swear to you. If you just go, I know nothing.

DANE (V.O.)
Alright. Come on home. You got ten minutes.

VINCENT
But you said --

DANE (V.O.)
-- I need to tie you with your wife to give me a head start. Hurry up.

SHERI (V.O.)
Don't come. He'll kill us both!

**Black on Vincent in Phonebooth**

**Lights Up on Ext. Vincent's Home**

Front yard of Vincent's Home - Sunrise Vincent, hobbles with a walking stick on his broken leg, entering the yard with the Levi jacket over his right hand holding the stick. The splint for his broken leg is held on by his Levi shirt sleeves.

He's in pain. But this isn't the defeated one-shoe, ragged suit peddler, Vincent Boyer who limped half shoeless into Driftwoods Crossing a dawn ago. This is a hardened Frenchman who faced his greatest fears twice and won... there to save his American family... or die trying.

Dane steps out of the shadows. Vincent turns slowly to find Dane holding a gun on him.

DANE
I told you not to start trouble, Frenchy. Now Quinnly and the others are dead, and you are the only one standing in my way of spending all that money. You see how it is, don't ya? Just you and me, with all I killed for between us.

VINCENT
Oui, and I'm sorry for the others. I just want to go inside, to make sure my wife is okay. You can tie me up, whatever works for you. You can still take the money and go far from here. I give you my word. As an honorable Frenchman. I'll never speak word of what happened between us. Ever.

DANE
Nah. You're still the loose end, Frenchy. You understand what that means?

VINCENT
Oui. Travis was very clear. With or without. As my father says, a single loose thread can ruin a perfectly handsome suit.

DANE
Suit? What suit?

VINCENT
My families business. You are my loose thread, no.

O.S. a COP SIREN fills the air. Dane turns his head.

DANE
What'd you...?

Vincent falls sideways SHOOTING the gun he took from Travis from under his Levi jacket.

HITTING Dane as Dane pulls his TRIGGER. Dane hits the ground backwards... hard.

Vincent's hand is to his face, as he lays there, blood seeping down under his glasses and over his face.

A tense moment. Both could be dead.

After a long pause, with the nightlife filling the void... Vincent's good leg finally twitches, than a finger on his gun hand.

He suddenly breathes with a gasp as though he had been underwater again. And fights the panic hard to sit up and get his head above it.

He sits there breathing hard, calming himself.

He adjusts his glasses, wiping the blood so he can see it's not water. He leans over and clears his throat.

Painful smile seeing Dane motionless.

VINCENT

At last, I am home. The winner. No?

The night fills with FLASHING cop lights and SIRENS

**Lights to Black.**

**CURTAIN**

www.ingramcontent.com/pod-product-compliance
Lightning Source LLC
Chambersburg PA
CBHW080553090426
42735CB00016B/3225

* 9 7 8 0 9 8 3 3 6 6 3 9 3 *